THE SIMPLE ROAD

THE SIMPLE ROAD

A Handbook for the Contemporary Seeker

OBADIAH HARRIS

JEREMY P. TARCHER/PENGUIN

An imprint of Penguin Random House | New York

JEREMY P. TARCHER/PENGUIN
An imprint of Penguin Random House LLC
375 Hudson Street
New York, New York 10014

Most Tarcher/Penguin books are available at special quantity discounts for
bulk purchase for sales promotions, premiums, fund-raising, and educational
needs. Special books or book excerpts also can be created to fit specific
needs. For details, write: SpecialMarkets@penguinrandomhouse.com.

Library of Congress Cataloging-in-Publication Data

Harris, Obadiah Silas.
The simple road : a handbook for the contemporary seeker / Obadiah Harris.
p.   cm.
Includes bibliographical references and index.
ISBN 978-0-399-17630-2
1. Spirituality.   2. Spiritual life.   I. Title.
BL624.H3325   2015   2015011719
204'.4—dc23

Printed in the United States of America
1   3   5   7   9   10   8   6   4   2

Book design by Lauren Kolm

CONTENTS

Introduction   The Road Before You   *ix*
               by Mitch Horowitz

THE ART OF SELF-HEALING

Chapter I   Sincerity, Receptivity & Retention   3

Chapter II   Creating a Body Open to Healing   7

Chapter III   The Physical Descent of Divine
               Consciousness   11

Chapter IV   The Mastery of Divine Consciousness   15

Chapter V   Cultivating Inner & Outer Strength   19

Chapter VI   Transformation of the Inner Self:
               Breaking the Habit of Frustration
               & Anxiety   23

OVERCOMING HOSTILE FORCES

Chapter VII   Facing Obstacles to Spiritual Growth   27

Chapter VIII   The Divine Life on Earth   29

Chapter IX   A Life Beyond Stress & Suffering   33

Chapter X   Upending the Hostile Forces   37

Chapter XI   Strengthening Weaknesses   41

Chapter XII   The Vanguard of Advancing Spiritual
                Consciousness   45

Chapter XIII   Defeating the Hostile Forces   49

THE MYSTERY OF WORK

Chapter XIV   The Lilies of the Field   53

Chapter XV   The Invisible Art of Inner Work   57

Chapter XVI   Releasing Oneself to Divine Will   61

THE PROBLEM OF FREE WILL

Chapter XVII   A Reconciliation of Contraries   67

Chapter XVIII   The Partisan Mind   71

Chapter XIX   Egoistic Free Will   75

Chapter XX   Psychic Free Will   79

SACRIFICE

Chapter XXI   The Self-Conscious Being of Man   85

Chapter XXII   The Transformative Sacrifice of
                Inner Purification   89

Chapter XXIII   Rejection of the Ego & Prioritization
                of the Soul   93

LIBERATION FROM GUILT

Chapter XXIV	What Is Guilt?	99
Chapter XXV	The Immorality of Theological Guilt	103
Chapter XXVI	Removing Theological Guilt	105
Chapter XXVII	Removing Personal Guilt: From Ignorance to Knowledge	109

FORGIVENESS

Chapter XXVIII	Understanding Forgiveness	115
Chapter XXIX	Forgiveness from the Heart	119
Chapter XXX	The Dangers of Ignorance	123
Chapter XXXI	Becoming a Vessel for Divine Truth	127
Chapter XXXII	The Strong Forgiver Is Thus Purified	131

LOVE

| Chapter XXXIII | The Perfect & the Imperfect | 137 |
| Chapter XXXIV | Psychic Love | 147 |

Notes	157
Bibliography	159
Index	161

Introduction

THE ROAD BEFORE YOU

by Mitch Horowitz

The book you are about to read could save your life. That is not some maudlin claim. I know it as fact—because it helped save mine.

Its author, Obadiah Harris, a university administrator, scholar of religion, and lifelong seeker, says little about himself. He makes hardly a personal reference throughout this book. So, before getting into what you will discover in this work—and defending the claim I make above—I will say something about the man behind it. Understanding the author and his background will illuminate how he reached his conclusions, and what they may hold for you.

Obadiah Harris was born on January 6, 1930, to an ardently Bible-reading family in Wynona, Oklahoma, a small town in the northeastern part of the state. His father was the pastor of a local Pentecostal church and his mother taught him to read using Scripture. They completed the entire Bible before Obadiah's first day of public school.

The Pentecostal faith was at the foundation of his household. Americans have long misunderstood Pentecostalism, with its emphasis on speaking in tongues and spiritual healing. The denomination is often viewed as belonging to the lower rungs of emotional religious life among the Southern poor; or, worse yet, critics see Pentecostals as a congregation of sheep who are exploited by slick televangelists and tent-revival faith healers.

In actuality, the Pentecostalism that animated Obadiah's childhood arose from a hunger among American Protestants to move beyond the formality and cold professionalism that had settled over much of mainline Christianity by the early twentieth century. Pentecostalism was not a call to flee the modern age but rather to revive a form of religion that intimately *mattered* in the life of the individual; a religion in which miracles, struggles against evil, and the peace brought by redemption were palpable forces. This was the faith in which Obadiah grew up: one of wonder, mystery, and commitment. Biblical figures were as real to his childhood as sports heroes and presidents.

When Obadiah was eight, a young Oral Roberts—then a freshly minted, twenty-year-old Pentecostal minister decades away from fame as a televangelist—conducted his first revival service at the elder Harris's church in Oil Center, Oklahoma. In person, Roberts was humble and gentle—but in the pulpit he burned with the conviction that religious healings and the ecstasies of the Holy Spirit had to be part of Christian faith if it was to remain relevant to modern people. Roberts's passions outstripped his experience: when he ran short of sermons, Obadiah's father gave him outlines for new ones.

As a teen, Obadiah followed his father on a circuit trail of churches, singing and accompanying himself on guitar. He became ordained as a Pentecostal minister, but yearned for greater freedom and opportunities. In particular, he wanted to broaden his religious perspective. The Judeo-Christian Bible was not, to his mind, the sole repository of religious truth. The notion that other, non-Christian faiths possessed Divine truth was intolerable within most Pentecostal circles—and the young minister was determined to move beyond them.

He began studying some of the new metaphysics that had gained popularity in America in the first half of the twentieth century, particularly the idea that the mind can serve as a channel of Divine creativity, and that thoughts possess causative properties. This outlook, generally called New Thought, went under the congregational banner of movements such as Science of Mind, Divine Science, and Unity. The philosophy's most articulate purveyors included Ernest Holmes, Charles and Myrtle Fillmore, and Neville Goddard—all of whom held, in their own way and with their own distinct emphases, that mental experience and spiritual experience were part of the same continuum, and that our feeling states and thoughts, and our capacity to direct these expressions along productive, generative lines, could manifest reality.

One day in early 1958, Obadiah was delivering a talk as a guest speaker at the Apostolic Christian Temple, a liberal evangelical congregation in Phoenix, Arizona. A slight bustle arose at the rear of the congregation when in walked a group of well-dressed, urbane-looking visitors. At the center of the group was a cheery-eyed, roundish man around whom the others gravitated—he was clearly their leader. Obadiah continued with his sermon, which dealt with the inner meaning of Christ's parables. The minister said that the parables were not intended as moral doctrine but as portraits of human archetypes, exposing our foibles and possibilities. At the end of the sermon the man at the center of the visitors walked up to Obadiah with a handshake and told him: "I enjoyed your talk. It was pure Science of Mind." This was Ernest Holmes, a figure Obadiah only dimly recognized from his studies, but who had assembled the most intellectually vibrant of the nation's New Thought congregations.

Holmes invited Obadiah to come to his Los Angeles seminary to study with him. "Don't try," Holmes said in a gentle but pressing manner, "just do it." Obadiah did go—and forged a close student-teacher bond with the metaphysical philosopher. By the late 1950s, Holmes had weathered bruising factional fights within his church and, with his health unsteady, he was searching for successors. He apparently found one in Obadiah, who was soon appointed senior minister at the First Church of Religious Science in Phoenix, one of the largest Science of Mind congregations at the time. He also spoke at Science of Mind churches up and down the West Coast.

In the late winter of 1960 Holmes was in markedly deteriorated health. Before his death on April seventh, the leader asked Obadiah to take over leadership of the Science of Mind movement. Obadiah declined. He had watched the movement and its factional politics consume too much of his mentor's life and energies. He knew that he once more had to leave a religious movement that he loved. "I have to find my own way," Obadiah told his teacher, kneeling by his sickbed. Holmes smiled and replied: "I wish I could go with you."

———

Obadiah did find his own way. He served until 1964 at the Phoenix church before pursuing a career in higher education. In 1973 he earned his doctor of philosophy in education at the University of Michigan in Ann Arbor. That year he became an associate professor of educational management and director of community education at New Mexico State University. Two years later he filled the same position at Arizona State University, where he remained for almost two decades, designing programs in community outreach, and in adult and continuing education. Obadiah's experience in diverse pulpits had given him the ability to communicate with wage-earning people who wanted to return to school; with retail, manufacturing, and railroad magnates who could fund new university programs; and with community members whom he wanted to bring into campus life for more than homecoming parades and football games.

In the early 1990s Obadiah's life path once again intertwined with an icon of American metaphysics, as it previously had with Ernest Holmes. This time it was with the legacy of a man who had died in 1990 and whom Obadiah had never personally met but knew by reputation: the esoteric scholar Manly P. Hall.

Although invisible to the mainstream, Hall had become the informal dean of the nation's alternative spiritual culture when at age twenty-seven in 1928 he independently published a massive codex to the mythical, symbolic, and occultic religious traditions of antiquity, *The Secret Teachings of All Ages*. The comprehensive *encyclopedia arcana* brought Hall sufficient resources from contributors to construct a "mystery school" in the Griffith Park neighborhood of Los Angeles, which he called the Philosophical Research Society. Hall's Egyptian-Mayan-Art Deco–styled campus grew to feature a world-class library of spiritual texts; a vault with ancient manuscripts and artifacts; a small complex of classrooms; book-production and warehousing facilities; and an auditorium. For seekers of esoteric wisdom, it was the closest thing to Valhalla.

But the place fell into financial ruin following Hall's death, when a series of legal disputes arose around his estate. The legal bills were crushing and resulted in the selling off of some of Hall's most treasured antiquities. The board brought in Obadiah as president in 1993 to set matters aright financially. He restored the organization to financial health and fulfilled one of Hall's aims by opening the University of Philosophical Research, an accredited, graduate degree–granting distance-learning college. In his more than twenty years on the job he has cashed no paycheck.

———

Those are the outer details of Obadiah's career—but this book returns him to the inner movements that undergird the outer; just as the outer helped inform the inner man. Obadiah's life has been marked not by random changes but by the need to yield to the demands of growth. To understand this requires casting one more look at the past before turning to the ideas in this book.

Although Obadiah could have pursued a career as Holmes's successor, and entered into a somewhat ready-made position of authority, he took a much longer road. This road not only avoided the trappings of religious politics, but it called to him for another reason—one that he rarely discusses and that I bring up here of my own choosing, not of his. Obadiah detected—rightly, in my view—a lack of intellectual excellence within much of the New Thought world following Holmes's death. There were, of course, outstanding ministers and personalities remaining in the movement; but there existed no new generation of thinkers who possessed Holmes's hunger to continually redefine New Thought principles and validate them in traditions ranging from the Vedas to Hermeticism to recent advances in mind-body medicine and physics. Figures such as Holmes and Neville Goddard were impeccable intellects whose reading habits ranged from Emerson and Blake to Mary Baker Eddy and Sri Aurobindo to studies in quantum physics and relativity. The New Thought movement, in Obadiah's view (and my own), failed to sustain a culture of intellectual vigor, in which seekers continually challenged and reformed old ideas in light of new discoveries, and the development of new religious cultures and expressions.

One of Obadiah's core points in this book is that religious thought has, in fact, changed over the course of centuries, and even in recent decades. The religious messenger is no longer a figure whose life is marked by martyrdom or persecution. The concept of guilt, he writes, does not serve modern people well, and is not foundational to Western religion. Guilt was not predominant in the earliest stirrings of the Mediterranean faiths that became Judaism and Christianity or in the Vedas—it grew from ancient judicial codes rather than mystical currents. Finally, the doctrinal approach to religion—in which the vision of a single faith dominates one's religious thought—may be losing its primacy in the Western world, even though that model has historically served as an incubator for invaluable ideas and insights.

Obadiah also insists on the continued relevance and possibility of miracles and wondrous events. He begins this book, bravely and unapologetically, with the subject of spiritual healings. That he opens the book in this way is notable; this is not a work that "hides its light under a bushel." Indeed, Obadiah's views on the possibility of healing through prayer and meditation point to continuity in his spiritual development. Some observers have difficulty understanding, or feel deep offense over, the emphasis on "signs and wonders"—and specifically miraculous healings—within Pentecostal, Charismatic, and certain Catholic congregations. Yet Obadiah has not rejected or run from the beliefs he grew up with; rather he has refined them, leavened them, and submitted their claims to the insights of other faiths, dramatic advances in medical science, and the caution that sudden healings and other remarkable events are matters of mystery and possibility, not outcomes that can be catered or predicted. Obadiah believes that if we categorically reject the possibility of the miraculous, we reduce what religion can offer the individual; we succumb to formalism and doctrine; we limit discovery.

But his approach will inevitably disappoint anyone in search of burning bushes, blinding flashes of insight, or quick fixes. Rather, he prescribes a lifetime of submission to Divine will, which means: persistent prayer, meditation, inner search and personal expansion through learning, immersion in diverse religious traditions, and the constant reestimation of one's values and motives. Obadiah encourages an awakening of the "educational variety," as described by philosopher William James. The simple road, as referred to in the title, is also the long road. Yet its path holds wonders to be discovered.

I began this introduction with my own bold claim: That this book was lifesaving to me. And so it was. It did not heal me of a physical malady or move a mountain out of my way. But it did reach me with a clear and simple truth, which shined a light forward for me when I was lost in a frightening and depressing personal struggle. Several months before I wrote this introduction, I was in a period of darkness after I felt that I had disappointed people I love. I knew that my actions were wrong and I couldn't figure out how I could have been so estranged from my own best instincts. I didn't want a way out of my problems—I wanted a way to understand them and to make amends to others.

Clarity came to me through reading Obadiah's chapters on "Overcoming Hostile Forces." He makes a challenging and immensely clarifying claim in that section: Namely, that we *do* face the presence of maleficent influences in this life—influences that seem to appear just when our self-assurance of "spiritual progress" may be at its zenith. At such times, he writes, these forces "have the right to test the sincerity of every spiritual devotee." They *have the right.* This is a very different perspective than merely viewing ourselves as plagued by evil or mischief-making spirits. Rather we are persistently—and necessarily—tested in life. This may be the meaning of an ancient parable found in both Judaism and Islam: When God expels Satan from heaven, the Creator whispers: *This way leads to me, too.*

Maleficent forces are sometimes self-produced. Obadiah writes of those individuals who "may subconsciously luxuriate in their misfortunes, deducing from them proof sufficient to their ego that all other people are at fault, and that fate is conspiring." In other instances people "consult the fortune-teller or sooth-sayer vainly seeking by superficial occult means to prevent these attacks which they can neither understand nor resist." This is an important passage: He is not denying the metaphysical basis of certain divinatory arts; nor is he condemning the classical occult tradition that arose from the Renaissance encounter with remnants of Greek, Roman, and Egyptian mystery religions. Instead, he is discouraging the kind of cheap grace that is sought through attempting to wishfully divine what lies on the road ahead, rather than accepting that road, bowing to its necessity, and strengthening our limbs for its challenges, which may require accepting and mending the calluses, sprains, or even broken bones that it may bring. Without these challenges we would stagnate; we would become permanently lost.

Some readers may object that not *all* tragedy can be understood as purposeful. We live in a world of war, disease, and appalling random violence. This is incontestably true. But we cannot make progress by arguing from extremes. Most of us, most of the time, face far more ordinary domestic and mundane challenges than bouts with ultimate evil. If we permit our concerns over extreme cases of evil to deter us from better understanding the circumstances that actually govern most of our workaday lives—circumstances that test rather than crush us—we will limit our ability to self search. We must start from where we are before we can begin to expand our perspective—that is the nature of "the simple road" toward which this book directs us.

For me personally, Obadiah's chapters on hostile forces helped reframe the struggle I was facing; these passages did not serve to lessen but to heighten my sense of bearing intimate, personal responsibility for my situation. It was necessary to engage my failures—and to try to emerge from them with a better sense of what I owed to others. My temptations to seek out reassurance by indulging in predictions, avoidance, or blame would do no good. And, yet, I also felt the odd and persistent sense that I was wrestling with a presence inside me that seemed totally unfamiliar; I was contending with something that felt alien. Was this some kind of a "hostile force"? Simultaneously—and I cannot emphasize this enough—the responsibility was wholly my own. This may sound paradoxical, but it has been suggested to me that living with paradox is a basic ingredient of spiritual inquiry.

———

Is the spiritual struggle even real? Can't everything I have just described be explained in psychological terms? Well, yes. But as

I and many seekers have discovered there is a point at which psychological insight brings us to water without quelling our thirst. Probing one's motivations does not always result in change; persistent self-reflection can set us on a repeat loop of morbid inner scrutiny that leads nowhere. My own crisis opened me to a period of deep prayer, which continues today. Indeed, this book calls us to prayer. We must finally appeal to the Higher to make us whole, to help us take steps that we cannot take by ourselves alone.

There exists a popular attitude today that we are self-sufficient as spiritual and ethical beings. A listener once asked philosopher Jacob Needleman: "Isn't everything that we need really inside us?" Needleman paused and responded, "Well, *there's a lot more in us than just that.*" In other words, we are shot through with forces, automatisms, habits, reactions, impulses, and negativities with which we are completely unfamiliar. We are in pieces. To pray is to seek alignment, to rely on something other than the mind as we conventionally use it.

This is where we can join in the suffering, joy, disappointment, and quest for understanding that has characterized the great religious expressions, from the Tao Te Ching to the Gospels to the Bhagavad Gita. These and other sources noted in this book give us a path to walk and methods to try. This is the *simple road* in the book's title; but it is also a greatly rigorous one.

When you grow exhausted with all of today's spiritual programs, axioms, seminars, and techniques; when you feel fatigued from searching and cannot find a way forward; when it seems that years of seeking have netted so little—throw yourself upon the essential truths in this book. Obadiah's work returns us to the foundation of the universal search as it exists in all of the historic faiths. This is a handbook for living. It calls us to the clear, revitalizing waters of faith. It can be lifesaving.

October 2014
New York City

MITCH HOROWITZ is a PEN Award–winning historian and the vice president and editor in chief at Tarcher/Penguin in New York. He has written on alternative spirituality for *The New York Times, The Wall Street Journal,* and *The Washington Post.*

THE ART OF SELF-HEALING

Chapter I

SINCERITY, RECEPTIVITY
& RETENTION

————

Those who believe in self-healing will find the way to heal themselves. This is not the way of the miraculous, but something experienced within and brought down from above. When Christ said, your faith will make you whole, he was referring to something that occurs within ourselves, and it is that something which we are seeking to discover.

What are the inner principles of healing which are generally grouped under the inclusive name of Faith? What are the components of the self-healing process? I call it self-healing because, as Christ said, it is something in which you have a part. To define this we can begin with three necessary steps, namely: sincerity, receptivity, and retention.

By sincerity is meant an earnest aspiration to the Divine Force for its restorative energy and healing power. We must not have this aspiration for selfish or egoistic purposes and ambitions, but to have health for divine purposes. We are not to get well just to go on with some mental or vital objective or work for our own ends and desires, or to boast of our healing, but for God's will and work in the world. We are not to aspire to spiritual healing for unspiritual purposes. Thus Christ, after healing someone, would say, go and sin no more, lest a worse thing come upon you.

The second step, receptivity, means an opening of all parts of our being to the descent of the Divine Force from above. This Force enters to heal, and must be admitted into every level of the physical mind, nerves, organs, and cells. No part or plane of us is to stand back stubbornly or dully, relying on itself alone, or inertly refusing to open and receive the Force. The body furnishes the most obstinate resistance and requires the greatest pressure for response.

The third step, retention, means to hold the Divine Force in us when it comes down. Often this seems too strong for us to bear. We sometimes are like a container that can receive only so much and spills the rest, or that has a break in it somewhere and loses as much as it receives. We become forgetful or wasteful of the Divine Grace after we have called for it. This must be avoided by preparing, purifying, and strengthening ourselves so that we will be a fit vessel, not only to receive but to retain the healing power. As the prophet Elisha told the widow woman, *We must have a clean vessel in which to receive the oil of the Lord.*

Chapter II

CREATING A BODY OPEN
TO HEALING

———

For this important step of retention to succeed, we must learn two things: cooperation and passivity. Cooperation requires a full and ready compliance with all sources and representatives that are available to help us in the healing. For instance, if you have a trusted spiritual guide through whom God is acting to heal you, give the divine representative your entire cooperation and pay heed to his advice. Ministers are often contacted by people seeking help in spiritual healing who not only will not cooperate, but actually resist spiritual advice. Remember that you are not only exerting your will to become well, but seeking to superimpose upon your will the Will of God for the rejection of the disease. So follow the Divine commands, however they are revealed to you. Although your part in this cooperation is the smaller, it is indispensable. Your consent to the healing must be given.

Let us now consider the passivity required. Passivity is as necessary as cooperation, but differs from it. In cooperation, you work with something. In passivity you are simply quiet before it, unmoving, unstirred. Let all parts and planes of your being be gravely passive, densely immobile, so that the divine healing power can work unobstructed in you. If a surgeon were operating on your body, you would be completely passive, anesthetized, unconscious on the table while operated upon. In spiritual healing, you must be even more passive so that God can do His healing work in you, without surgery and without medication, without the knife or the needle. Your passivity to God is not mechanical, drugged, or unconscious. It is a conscious passivity from the inside and not from the outside. It is much stronger and gives a better ground for the healing work than any anesthetic and leaves no scars on your body. Cooperation and passivity are especially necessary in serious cases.

The passivity will permit the tremendous life and energy of the Infinite to flow into you from above. Let this flow to the diseased organ or part of the body affected. The power and light from above will clear up the congestion of the nerves in the affected areas. This will permit the normal processes of nutrition, discarding of diseased tissue, and rebuilding and restoration of health.

Chapter III

THE PHYSICAL DESCENT OF
DIVINE CONSCIOUSNESS

———

Thus far those things have been listed which come under the heading of faith and will, such as sincerity, receptivity, retention, cooperation, and passivity. But another element is imperative and dynamic.

The Divine consciousness must descend into the physical. There it will meet and dethrone the hostile opposition of disease. This is dramatically symbolized in the New Testament by the casting out of devils from the sick through the power of Christ. The illness, symbolized by the devils, always enters us from the outside, through some imperfection or weakness, or opening to adverse touches in our physical nature. Once they are in, they try to entrench themselves. We call through the soul for the Divine Power to enter into us, to cast out the disease that has got into us through the weaknesses of our lower nature. The disease enters from the outside; the Healing Power descends from above. In a sense, we are the battleground where the Divine Commander conquers the disease.

Consciousness of the Divine in the physical eliminates disease. In my flesh shall I see God, said Job. To have this consciousness, not just in mind or heart, but in the cells of the body, is to develop the power of stopping disease. As this stopping capacity increases, you can control transient illness and rid yourself of chronic disease which has become settled in your body. You must, however, allow time for this process. It is enough at first to halt the spread of the disease. Then you can gradually make headway against it, consolidate your gains, and finally throw it out altogether. Patience and persistence are necessary; follow a little progress with more progress. Do not be discouraged by a temporary setback. You will recover any lost ground and forge ahead to a new conquest of territory. Miracles should not be demanded. Instant healing may sometimes occur in the highly developed or through unusual faith—that faith which moves mountains, as Christ said; but most of us must be prepared for a comprehensible process in which the time required must be allowed to elapse.

The object is not to discover the most efficient way of healing so much as it is to change the entire consciousness, including the physical, to the end that illness cannot come at all. Our entire being must be so transformed that illness becomes impossible. The aim is not only to lift us from the agonies of the sickbed, but to keep us out of the sickbed, the hospital, and the doctor's office.

In a sense, medical science reflects these dual aspects of healing. That is, medical science divides itself into curative medicine and preventive medicine. The first to heal, and the second to fend off disease—to keep you from catching or having it. Medical prevention is by medical measures, while spiritual immunization is by spiritual measures and is the more powerful, although medical prevention is not to be ignored. It is a fact that most people found in doctors' offices today are there because they are sick already, not to prevent sickness. The same is true of ministers. Sick people go to their pastor for spiritual help when they are already ill, and not to learn the secret of spiritual immunity to disease. Their best hope is to get immediate relief and continue as they are—to become armored against future illness altogether is generally not in their minds.

Chapter IV

THE MASTERY OF DIVINE CONSCIOUSNESS

We should have a practical understanding of the place of medical healing and of spiritual healing, and their relationship to each other. If you are not yet spiritually strong enough to heal yourself, or to immunize yourself against illness, you should not hesitate to call on doctors and medical science to help you. If you break your leg, you need a doctor to set it. This is an accident and not an organic illness. Common sense must be used. One should not go to the extreme on one hand of casting the doctor into limbo, or on the other of excluding the most powerful of all healing forces, the spiritual. There are also influences such as heredity, environment, kinds of food, and others that enter into the state of health, and one should not neglect these aspects. But the psychological is the most important. It is through the psyche that we aspire to the Divine Force, and through the psyche the Force descends to heal us.

All apathy and resignation to disease must be avoided. Have the courage to master it. Some people consider that illness induces a spiritual turn in their lives. It is true that illness, like any other misfortune, sometimes initiates such a turn; but actually the turn is due to a deeper disposition already present in our nature. Many people are ill without too much change in their spiritual attitude, and some without any. In fact, some become unhappy and bitter about their illness. So sickness is not to be given undeserved laurels as a way to become spiritual. In reality, it is by the spiritual that we unlock the grasp of sickness upon us. Illness is an imperfection in the body, as ignorance is an imperfection of the mind, or instability in the nervous system. All of these imperfections must be conquered through the power of the Spirit.

Some people believe in and practice faith healing by the laying-on of hands. You have perhaps seen this firsthand on television, if not in the tents of the itinerant evangelist, and occasionally in very staid and formal churches. I am not deprecating this kind of healing for it is of help to some people, as I have seen with my own eyes. Blind faith has been known to clear up physical difficulties, but there is a higher spiritual healing than the mere physical act of laying on hands. By attempting to attain a Divine consciousness in the body for its transformation, and thereby encompassing the preparations, conditions, and methods necessary, it is possible not only to cure, but to immunize ourselves against disease. That is why Christ said, "Your faith has made you whole,"[1] rather than any outer physical gesture. This is what Sri Aurobindo calls a conscious conquest of the physical nature by the Power of the Spirit.[2]

That is why it is important to learn how we can spiritually control, check, and defeat disease and become immune to it. For this, Divine Grace is the dynamic element, and complete cooperation and passivity are necessary so that the Force can work in us to heal. We must not resign ourselves to illness, but conquer it and set up new frontiers that it can never cross again.

Let us have calm confidence in the Divine healing power and in God's protection, as the centurion did—the Roman soldier who said to Christ that he need not visit his home to heal his servant, but that if only Christ would speak the word he was certain his servant would be healed. And Christ marveled, saying, "I tell you, not even in Israel have I found such faith."[3] Let us have such faith and we, too, shall be healed by the word of God.

Chapter V

CULTIVATING INNER & OUTER STRENGTH

———

The sick person tends to accumulate difficulties other than just their illness. For instance, they can no longer do their work well, and this creates additional problems. These, too, can be conquered. On the other hand, the individual who is beset with life problems that have nothing to do with disease may come down with some sickness because of stress; so we must unravel the problem of nonsickness difficulties in order to be safe against them also. Those who believe that they will be victorious over such difficulties will discover the way to banish them. That discovery is the object of this book.

Let us realize at the outset that the problem has two aspects.

The first is the difficulty itself, which always comes from the outside and may be any variety of hostile outer circumstances or events—financial, mental, social, or otherwise. The second is your inner condition; that is, any defects or weaknesses in you which are disturbed by the outer difficulty. The rule to apply is that the inner defect must be transformed and the outer difficulty shut out through Divine Grace. What happens outside must not be permitted to disturb you; what is within you must be strengthened where it is weak. To become strong and quiet inwardly you must be invulnerable outwardly. You must refuse to allow your inner being to rush here and there every time something adverse attacks you from the outside; nor should you have any feelings of depression because of difficulties. There is no cause for depression. Difficulties occur in all endeavors, including the spiritual, and to all people as well as yourself. There is no reason to doubt your eventual victory or the efficacy of the Divine Grace on your behalf.

Every time you defeat a difficulty, you will be stronger to gain new triumphs. You should note any defect in you, not with self-disparagement or despondency, but in a positive way. Concentrate on how to get rid of it, on what you are to become and not what you have been. Sri Aurobindo says there are two ways of overcoming difficulty: the first, or negative way, is to reject the difficulty, which always comes from the outside. The second, or positive way, is to bring down the light, peace, and purity from above to replace the inner defects with a Higher Consciousness. In this descent you will develop your inner realization until it becomes so strong that the roots of weakness in you have no soil in which to grow and are pulled up by a spontaneous psychic change.

Do not consider that your inner defects are such that they cannot be mastered. Every inner weakness can be gradually overcome. It is the attacks from the outside that you must close off so that they do not affect you; no progress can be made otherwise. As to inner defects, when a weakness presents itself, look upon it as an occasion to see what defect in you remains to be dealt with—the unfinished business of your transformation. Call down Power and Light to dig the defect out of yourself. This should be done with no emotional excitement and with a steady and calm rejection of the difficulty, and a constant and quiet calling down of the Divine Force. The inner nature must be transformed and the outer difficulty refused admittance. From the inner conquest comes the outer victory. When you are strengthened and changed within, nothing outside can disturb you. You will be master of yourself and of your surroundings.

The rule to remember is to reject the outer attack and transform the inner weakness. Exert your will and call on the Divine Grace to get this done. If you do not call on Divine Grace, you will be like the man of whom Christ spoke about; the man began to build a tower but was not able to finish it, and all who beheld it began to mock him.

Chapter VI

TRANSFORMATION OF THE INNER SELF: BREAKING THE HABIT OF FRUSTRATION & ANXIETY

––––––––

Do not be discouraged or impatient if, for a time, you continue to have the old mechanical inner reactions of frustration and anxiety when a fresh difficulty presents itself. These reactions are only a habit which can be broken, like any other habit. The outer attacks, while they are met everywhere in ordinary life, are especially trying to the spiritual seeker. The higher you go on the spiritual path, the greater the attack. That is why the spiritually advanced cannot bear the slightest imperfection and suffer the most from the least impurity in themselves. The spiritual is the highest of all goals, and the difficulties you meet on this path are more serious than in any other; but if your dedication to the Divine is sincere, you will pass safely over them all.

As a university professor, administrator, and faculty and student advisor, I have had people come to me for help with a swarm of external life problems: jobs, marriage, financial, and others by which they say they are bewildered. Often it is extremely difficult to get the minds of such people who need help away from these preoccupations. They are so engrossed with what they want on the outside that it is next to impossible to turn their attention within. They only think: Give me what I want on the outside and I will be inwardly content and quiet, not realizing that only when they are inwardly content and calm will everything on the outside be right for them. They have a sentimental, nervous weakness in the system, and a refusal to recognize and change the inner defects.

In an effort to provide effective counsel to such people, often I am compelled to say: I cannot help you until you are willing to shut off these outer hostile pressures, and set out on the path of self-transformation, for anything that I can tell you will mean nothing unless you become different from what you now are.

OVERCOMING HOSTILE FORCES

Chapter VII

FACING OBSTACLES TO SPIRITUAL GROWTH

———

Great individuals have always faced great difficulties. Job, in the Old Testament, said to his companion as they faced the battle, "Be of good courage . . . and God will do what seems good to Him."[4] Christ was frank and realistic with his disciples about the difficulties they would face. "Behold," he said, "I send you out as sheep in the midst of wolves; so be as wise as serpents and innocent as doves. Beware of men; for they will deliver you up to councils and will flog you . . . and you will be dragged before governors and kings for my sake . . . You will be hated by all for my sake. But he who endures to the end will be saved . . . If they have called the master of the house Beelzebub, how much more will they malign those of his household. So have no fear of them; for nothing is covered that will not be revealed, or hidden that will not be known."[5]

Thus did Christ portray the difficulties that hostile forces of darkness would bring against his followers. Sri Aurobindo, in our day, describes them also. He says that the hostile forces have a certain self-chosen function. They serve to make the aspirant ready for the spiritual descent and transformation. At every step of the journey they are there, attacking furiously; criticizing; suggesting, imposing, responding to, or inciting revolt; raising unbelief; and amassing difficulties. No doubt these forces put a very exaggerated interpretation on the rights given them by their function, making mountains out of what seems to us a molehill. A little false step or mistake and they appear on the road and clap a whole Himalaya as a barrier across it. But this opposition has been permitted from of old, not merely as a test or ordeal, but as a compulsion for us to seek a greater strength, a more perfect self-knowledge, and purity, and force of aspiration, a faith that nothing can crush, a more powerful descent of the Divine Grace.[6]

Chapter VIII

THE DIVINE LIFE
ON EARTH

———

There are three unrealistic views in vogue today that hinder the individual and society in overcoming their problems. The first is the religious position that disposes of the question of conquering difficulties by saying that it cannot be done. Only in another world, in some nirvana, or a distant paradise beyond death can difficulties be dissolved. Dr. Albert Schweitzer has written that this pessimistic outlook is found in some of the orthodox theology of two of the world's great religions, Christianity and Buddhism. In both of these theologies there is love and compassion for man, but no hope for him in the world. I say theological outlook, because Christ himself uttered no such teaching or doctrine. "Difficulties there will be," he said, "do not shrink or fly from them, but endure them and you will be delivered." "Fear not, little flock," he said, "it is your Father's good pleasure to give you the kingdom"[7]—the kingdom that is to come on earth as it is in heaven. Christ was not speaking of another world, or only of an inner world, but of heaven and earth as one.

Second, there is another religious view which is more modern but equally unrealistic. This second view is that there are no difficulties. Man is perfect, life has no problems, nothing needs changing; there is no evolution because perfection is already here.

If such were the case, this discussion would be unnecessary. The churches could close their doors; the hospitals could be boarded up; the local police dismissed; the courts abolished; and all our military forces, both here and abroad, could lay down their arms and return to their homes. This theory is born of confusion as to the relationship of the soul, mankind, and the world. The soul within us is perfect, but the outer life of the individual and its collective or communal life in the world is not yet perfect; it is advancing or evolving toward perfection. The world is not a dream and neither is it incapable of perfection.

The third view is a variation of the first, and also invalid. It considers this a world in which mankind cannot solve its difficulties and would not be disposed to do so even if it could. Therefore, there is little or no use in pursuing great ideals and noble aims, such as peace in the world and unity among nations, the kingdom of God on earth. These are the fantasies of visionaries or of messianic delusion. In this view mankind is naturally disposed to evil purposes. It is marked by Original, unchangeable sin. This outlook declares that many create their own difficulties because of indolence, shiftlessness, inherent sinfulness, and ignorance, and preferring these conditions, would not improve if they had the opportunity. This view encourages separateness, egoism, greed, and pride. It often directly intervenes to block men from rising above difficulties by refusing them encouragement, aid, or sympathy. It challenges the objectives of a better order for all and declares impossible the abundant life and the peace and liberation for which Christ said that he came.

All such views must be rejected. We must look upon all our individual difficulties as surmountable within and without, and we must do likewise with respect to our collective difficulties. Let there be the Divine Life on earth, and perfect man in a perfect society. The prophet Ezekiel asked, "How shall these things be?" And God replied, "I will give them one heart, and put a new spirit within them . . . and they shall be my people and I will be their God."[8]

Chapter IX

A LIFE BEYOND STRESS & SUFFERING

———

All men in their endeavors encounter from time to time hostile forces that oppose their efforts and try their perseverance and courage. They must either defeat or fall under the sway of these forces, become their masters or their victims.

It is our object to learn the secret of the complete conquest. Some people attain a partial mastery and, to a corresponding extent, become immune to hostile attacks. To that degree they enjoy peace. At the lowest stage of resistance are those persons who rarely, if ever, are able to repel the attacks, each of which is as annoying or injurious to them as its predecessor, if not more so. One day it may be a quarrel, on the next an economic reverse;

then perhaps an illness, a disappointment, disillusionment, or failure of some kind. Such individuals grow to live in daily expectation of dire events. They may subconsciously luxuriate in their misfortunes, deducing from them proof sufficient to their ego that all other people are at fault, and that fate is conspiring against them. It is impossible for anyone to make spiritual headway while possessed of this disposition. Every trace of it should be removed from the spiritual aspirant.

Disastrous indeed are the effects upon individuals who are caught in this net, and do not extricate themselves from it. Some become panic-stricken and live in what Thoreau called a quiet desperation. Others may become embittered, cynical, satirical, defiant, or irreligious. Or in search of some relief from the cloud that seems to hang over them, they dash from one religion to another. Or they consult the fortune-teller and the soothsayer, vainly seeking by superficial occult means to prevent these attacks which they can neither understand nor resist. As the Biblical proverb goes, "The wicked flee when no one pursues."[9]

However formidable these hostile forces may have been, they can be overcome, even by those who have suffered the most and the longest from them. This can be done yet most readily and speedily by those who have had a degree of success in holding off the attacks and are, therefore, not so vulnerable.

To achieve a complete victory over the hostile forces, it is necessary to learn three things: First: What they are; Second: How they attack; Third: How to defeat them. Religion has long considered this problem to be within its province. In fact, next after devotion to God, whose force is good and supreme, religion has sought to protect man against the satanic or hostile forces which are evil and subordinate. Modern psychology has aided by contributing scientific knowledge concerning the stress caused by such attacks and the resultant damage which they cause to the human system.

Chapter X

UPENDING THE HOSTILE FORCES

———

Let us now take up the first point: What are the hostile forces? We must identify them before we can contain and repel them. The classic example, in religion, of a test imposed on man by the dark forces is the Book of Job in the Bible. Here the opponent is Satan, the hostile forces at their metaphysical summit, for Satan is named in Job as one of the sons of God.

God says that Job is a blameless, upright man who fears God and does no wrong. Satan asks, "Does Job love God for nothing? You have given him every blessing a man could want. Take these from him and he will curse you to your face." God answers by giving Satan permission to test Job, subject to one condition:

"all that he has is in your power; only do not stretch out your hand against him."[10]

In the ensuing encounter, hostile forces of one kind or another assail Job. He loses his children, his possessions, and his health, but he holds fast to his integrity and his trust in God. He proves that he is not a man bought by God with favors. The most subtle hostile attacks come from those closest and dearest to him. His own wife tells him to curse God and die, but Job will not. His three best friends charge him with some secret sin, and plead with him to repent, that he may merit the forgiveness of the Lord. But Job, like God, knows that he is blameless, and answers them with superb sarcasm. "No doubt you are the people," says Job to his friends, "and wisdom will die with you. But I have understanding as well as you; I am not inferior to you."[11]

However, in his sorrow and suffering, Job displays one weakness, one revolt. He does not curse God, but he curses the day he was born. In the end, God rebukes Job for thus being weak, although He rebukes Job's three friends far more severely for being wrong. God then restores to Job everything and more that had been taken from him, and Job had honor and abundance as never before.

Job was a figure of magnificent faith and courage in his unflinching trust in God. Is it possible for us to be strong where he was weak? Can we win in his victory without undergoing the depth of his distress? If Job had devoted less time to cursing the day he was born, and more to defeating the devil, could he have had more success against the hostile forces? If we can avoid his weakness, will we avoid for ourselves the rebuke that God administered to Job?

The Book of Job was written thousands of years ago. Man's spiritual knowledge has advanced since then. If we could write a new Book of Job in our day, and in it depict and experience the entire victory of man over the hostile forces, should we not do so? Shall we not refuse to give our assent to the losing of anything to the hostile forces, either our trust in God, our health, or our other blessings?

Shall we not hold fast to an integrity greater yet than that of Job, and say to the hostile forces: I do not consent to give you a foothold in me, and I will not curse the day I was born. With God's help I shall stand fast against you and repel you at every quarter. I shall find how you launch your attacks and how to thwart them. I shall shore up my defenses where they are weak, steady my nerves, strengthen my body, deepen my understanding, and above all, call on the spiritual Power from within and above to crush your dark legions. If you call in demons, I shall call in angels. If you seek to ruin my health, I shall find spiritual ways to throw your poisons out of my body. If you seek to make me weep, I shall instead rejoice in the glory of God.

Chapter XI

STRENGTHENING WEAKNESSES

———

In a sense, we are today like Job talking with his friends, but our talk is in a different vein. We are not concerned with proving or disproving that Job was a sinner. That is the concept of a past religious era, and religious truth advances with the ages. What we are concerned with is how to make ourselves immune to the classic sufferings of Job, not to cover ourselves with sackcloth and ashes, but with the garments of joy, and the vindication of the spirit.

It is our task not to let the hostile forces toy with us as something we cannot fathom or resist, but to become their master and to shield ourselves from their wounds. If we could do this, people would come from far and wide to see us, not as they did to see Job in the midst of his afflictions of disease, sorrow, and poverty, but in the midst of health, bliss, and abundance. And God, at the end of our test, would commend us even more highly than He did Job, and rebuke those who disputed our course. Job would have been the first to say, spare yourself what I endured.

With this objective before us, let us pass now to our second point: We must know how the hostile forces attack so that we can first blunt the attacks and then repel them altogether.

We have seen that in the economy of existence there is an eternal opponent who attacks us whenever our movements are improper, our motives impure, or our weaknesses unremedied. The opponent does not attack because he is good or his purposes good. He may not only be hostile, but vicious, probing vengefully for a weak spot in our defenses. He may be an unworthy enemy supporting an unrighteous cause, yet it turns out for our benefit. If we are in error, the hostile force will give us a fall and thus indirectly help to make us realize our mistake and correct it. The effect is thus the same. It is our own actions and motives that must be changed for we cannot lay these against the hostile force which is not there to change. That is why, in some metaphysics, the hostile force is called the "left hand of God," and why, in the Book of Job, Satan is named as among "the sons of God."[12]

We must put aside all self-pity, self-reproach, and self-cursing. This, in itself, facilitates the attack against us. Remember what

God said to Job: "Shall a fault-finder contend with the Almighty? Anyone who argues with God must respond."[13] Instead we should calmly and dispassionately look within ourselves to discover where our weakness is, and where we are giving way. These vulnerable points should then be strengthened and made attack proof.

Next we should observe from what direction or source the outer attacks are coming so that we can guard against them. Usually the source is in an old weakness with which the outer hostile agency makes contact. Suppose, for instance, that we have struggled against, and for the most part succeeded, in overcoming frequent or uncontrollable anger. Suddenly some person or event catches us off guard and we burst out in a fit of anger. It mushrooms within us like a psychological atom bomb, consuming all in its path. Calmness flees and judgment falters. We are unable to meditate or pray. The stress malforms our organs and glands, pollutes the bloodstream, and activates or reactivates disease.

That is how the attack starts. It is the response or assent of an inner weakness to an outer attack. The remedy is to detect the condition immediately and rectify it. Stop the response of anger within and reject the attack from outside. This is all that is necessary; but vigilance is required. One cannot go around in a fog of self-conceit, in a blithe egoistic disregard of weaknesses in oneself that have not yet been fully conquered. If one does fall into this fog, there will come a moment when consciousness is lowered or vigilance relaxed. Suddenly the weakness flares up and the attack begins all over again. It can also arise from a hidden weakness, the presence of which one is not aware.

How do we avoid a lowering of our consciousness? As one sage says, we should, instead, develop the cosmic consciousness—let the egocentric outlook disappear in wideness, impersonality, the sense of the Cosmic Divine, the perception of universal forces, and the realization and understanding of the cosmic manifestation.[14]

Chapter XII

THE VANGUARD OF ADVANCING
SPIRITUAL CONSCIOUSNESS

We should not permit ourselves to be swept away by every changing circumstance that the ego seizes upon with its clamors and apprehensions. If we are accustomed to fly to pieces whenever some obstacle or affront presents itself, our self-control and self-command vanish. These are merely mechanical nervous responses, habitual reactions. You can cultivate an opposite, undisturbed outlook and firmly retain your composure.

As the ancient Taoist proverb says, count wherever you live as a good place to dwell. There may be added: Count your friends and associates as those with whom it is good to be; See God beneath every semblance and in every demeanor. This will give you the proper attitude. Regardless of where you are or whom you are with, you will never lose your self-possession. Instead of stress, you will have contentment. Instead of sickness, you will enjoy health. Instead of falling victim to the hostile forces, you will be their conqueror.

Occasionally or momentarily you may have lapses into the old weaknesses. At such moments what is necessary is to apply again the remedy of detecting and rejecting. If the old waves of remorse start to well up again, remind yourself that they are spies and subversives within that will betray you to hostile forces without. Cease all such withering self-reproaches. Do not become obsessed or preoccupied with the inner weaknesses or the outer attacks, and think and talk of nothing else. Instead, remember the good strides you have made already on the spiritual path, and that your victory is assured in the end.

You may wonder, at such times, why, if you have made considerable progress, such lapses should occur to give you a momentary setback. Why, you may ask, do I have to refight these old battles within myself? It is because you represent the vanguard of advancing spiritual consciousness. The hostile forces concentrate their onslaught upon you precisely for this reason. You have not only advanced yourself, but in you is much of the hope of the future, a light and an example from the Divine that other men may follow safely for the general conquest of the forces of darkness and ignorance in the world. The hostile forces must try to attack you or they lose all.

The hostile forces exist to keep up the ignorance in the world. They do not want it to diminish or cease. As such they have the right to test the sincerity of every spiritual devotee. They test our strength and our will to overcome every obstacle on the path to the Divine; but that is only until the Divine Light has descended into all our being, into mind, emotions, and finally into the body, that last stubborn redoubt of the physical whose inertia and obscurity cause it to be the last to surrender to God. Then our paths will be easy and trouble-free. It will be a progressive development and not a struggle every inch of the way.

Chapter XIII

DEFEATING THE HOSTILE FORCES

———

We have already touched on this point in passing, but not as much as necessary, for to defeat the dark forces is not easy. All of the conditions must be met. A proper attitude is essential; one that is psychic, unegoistic, and receptive only to the Divine. If this attitude can be taken and kept, your progress will be much more rapid. You can work toward the change in yourself. You can turn from egoism to the truth and the light. These are the conditions that must be satisfied and the help that is needed. As long as any egoism remains in the nature, it is the Trojan horse through which the hostile attacks pierce the walls of our defense. Especially to be avoided, when you have made a measure of progress, is any tendency toward spiritual vanity or self-righteousness, or assuming a superior, holier-than-thou attitude toward others. This invites the fiercest of all attacks.

A constant, calm working and avoidance of all impatience, impetuosity, hurry, or indolence is necessary. Aspire to the Divine with a quiet, steady working to bring realization from within and above. Observe the changes within yourself, where they occur, how far they extend, where they lead to the highest. At every moment there should be openness to the Divine Force to dissolve all darkness and unconsciousness in your nature and to assure victory.

"Deck yourself with majesty and dignity," said God to Job; "Clothe yourself with glory and splendor . . . look on everyone that is proud and abase him; look on everyone that is proud and bring him low; and tread down the wicked where they stand. Hide them in the dust together . . . Then will I acknowledge that your own right hand can give you the victory."[15]

Thus it is to God that we must turn for victory over vain and wicked forces. Thus did Christ say, "Come to me, all ye who are weary and heavy-laden and I will give you rest . . . Take my yoke upon you and learn of me, for I am gentle and lowly in heart, and you will find rest for your soul, for my yoke is easy and my burden is light."[16] If we aspire for the power and presence of the Divine in our hearts, the yoke of the adversary will be removed from us, and we will find rest for our soul in the peace of God.

THE MYSTERY OF WORK

Chapter XIV

THE LILIES OF THE FIELD

———

Within the changes that take place in the life of the spiritual seeker, a new attitude toward work usually occurs. Some think that the ideal in work would be to give it up altogether and become absorbed in spiritual purification exclusively. They long to get away from the marketplace, office, or the shop into the clear and lofty atmosphere of the spirit, far above all lower clouds, storms, and strivings.

Others are willing enough, and even desirous of working, but find that their work disturbs them, and consequently impedes their spiritual endeavor. They earnestly aspire to be spiritual but often ask how they can do so when they must devote so much time to work, and be so exhausted or upset by their labors.

The problem of action or inaction has long been a metaphysical question. In ancient times ascetics found as their solution to this problem a renunciation of work and the world. They begged for their food and lived in caves and forest huts. This extreme practice has waned, but vestiges of its influence remain.

There is a haunting attitude in the West, for example, that to be a Christian means to be poverty-stricken. Christ gave no such teaching, and nowhere advised men against work. "The laborer," he said, "is worthy of his wages."[17]

The Christian scriptures are plain enough on this point, but the Apostle Paul, in particular, has been misconstrued in this connection, largely because Paul places so much emphasis on faith instead of works; but the works that Paul rejected were works of the Hebraic law, such as strict ceremonial regulations about what to eat, when to wash the hands, and so forth, which of themselves could save no one.

Paul was as blunt as anyone could be about the necessity of work. "If anyone will not work," he said, "let him not eat."[18] Yet there is a mystery in work which Christ intimated when he said, "Consider the lilies of the field: they neither toil nor spin. Yet Solomon in all his glory was not arrayed like one of these."[19] This seems to say that God clothed the lilies in beauty by his power and without toil on their part. If we call upon God's power to do our work, then it is done by us as though it were not toil at all, and in beauty.

The Bhagavad Gita, India's most highly regarded scripture, is largely concerned with this problem of work. It teaches that all work should be done without regard to the fruits of the action, and as a sacrifice to God. In this way, the Gita declares, all egoistic clamor for rewards of work will be stilled, and the worker will be disturbed neither by success nor failure, profit or loss, repute or disrepute. His dependence will be on God, the imperishable.

If I work only to satisfy my own demands, I have not found the divine Truth. If I do not work in order to find the Divine Truth, it eludes me. If I find the Divine Truth and do what it commands, then I have also discovered the secret of work. What work I then do will be appropriate, productive, and effective. It will not be done partially or inadequately, nor will it be done without regard for others, but in harmonious concert with all. It will bring wholesomeness, abundance, light, and grace to mankind.

The Psalms utter the words of God: "If I ascend into heaven, You are there; if I make my bed in hell, behold, You are there. If I take the wings of the morning, and dwell in the uttermost parts of the sea, even there Your hand shall lead me, and Your right hand shall hold me."[20] Surrender the responsibility for your work to the Omnipresent Divine, do the work for Him as His instrument, see that He is doing the work through you and your work will be perfect and beautiful, like the lilies of the field.

This perfection in work will not come to you all at once, but in time, as you learn more and more not to shirk or spoil what work you are to do, and do it willingly and well, as a sacrifice to God. Whatever work you then do proceeds from the Divine Truth you have discovered and not from selfish choice or egoistic preference.

Chapter XV

THE INVISIBLE ART OF
INNER WORK

———

Work is necessary to a balanced life. Through work our inner progress is expressed in our outer nature and activity. Both should be full of the Divine. Our outer life is thus purified; at the same time, outer experience in work helps to develop the will and power of our inner being.

Paul said that he was shipwrecked, imprisoned, stoned, and left for dead. These experiences strengthened his faith and his faith enabled him to go through them safely.

All that we do may be divided into inner work and outer activity. With outer work we are familiar. It is those efforts and labors by which man's external life is conducted, regulated, and sustained. It is reconstructed and rearranged from time to time by changes in laws and customs, as the times and the progress and good of the human race may require. This is the work of the leaders, teachers, artisans, and evolving people everywhere. Thus, outer work is necessary to the life of all and cannot be neglected.

With inner work we are less familiar. Yet it is primary and even more important not to neglect. The inner invisible work is the spiritual force by which the individual decisively influences external work and human conditions. This Inner Force concretely and beneficially affects all realms of human activity: cultural, educational, familial, and political. It is a more powerful force than any which science can summon. The individual can exert this Inner Force silently and invisibly, even to those whom this Inner Work is helping. When doing so, one works with universal forces not apparent in surface events, yet determining their outcome for the right and the good.

The greatest spiritual seers of mankind—the Christs and the Buddhas—have always worked primarily from the Inner Force. They did not hold private or official positions of any kind in outer activities; but their influence on human happiness greatly exceeds that of those who do external work exclusively or mainly. It was with this meaning that Christ answered Pilate: "My kingdom is not of this world; if my kingdom were of this world then would my servants fight . . . but my kingdom is not from hence."[21] Thus Christ said that his kingdom came from within, from the

Inner Spiritual Force which is far more effective and tangible in its results than the strongest physical power that science and technology have produced or may discover.

Let us understand clearly that the inner work of which we are speaking does not abandon life, but puts it upon a spiritual basis. It works toward the perfection of external life to its greatest extent as the manifestation of inner spiritual realization.

Chapter XVI

RELEASING ONESELF TO
DIVINE WILL

————

Some may ask, How does one go about such spiritually based inner and outer work? How does one dedicate all his activities to the Divine? What are the day-by-day and moment-by-moment steps to take?

There are several helpful methods. You need not be so constantly preoccupied with your dedication that you cannot work for reminding yourself of it. You can remember that you are doing your work for the Divine at the start of the work, and give thanks to God at the end, or during breaks in your work. This is good as a beginning. Or you can work in a kind of dual consciousness, one with which you are working and the other with which you are detached and intensely conscious of the divine dedication of the work you are doing.

Another way is to become aware that God is doing the work through you as an instrument; then God, and not your mental idea or personal will, is in charge, and your consciousness is quiet and passive in the Divine. The quickest and most effective way, however, is a simple constant aspiration and complete will of consecration to God, in which you call upon the Divine Power to do the work. You should expect, however, that even this simplest way will take time to achieve.

"Study," the Apostle Paul said, "to show thyself approved unto God."[22] You may find yet other ways. It is not the method that is all-important, but that you should be always open to the Divine Force. The great secret of work is to know how to get things done by the Divine Power above, and not by your mental effort alone.

As one philosopher has said, it is the power of this inner work descending from the Divine Truth above which will create a new life upon the earth for the whole of mankind. Such a power which will create a new life and a new society is not likely to be received at first by humanity as a whole. It will be received at first only by a few, and from them it will gradually spread over the rest of the world. Those who do receive it will serve as models for the rest of humanity to mold their lives likewise. This will eventually create a new humanity born again, as Christ said they must be. It will bring harmony, unity, liberation, and peace on earth.

This is the noble destiny of man. All of us should make this the model of our work; then our outer work will bear the stamp of inner perfection in the power and grace of God by Whom the work is given, and for Whom it is done in truth and joy, in beauty and in love.

In this discussion we have shown that the work of man as it affects human society is both inner and outer, and that the inner work is primary. We have emphasized that the inner work is undertaken not to neglect or abandon the outer work, but to perfect it. We have pointed out that it was because the Christs and the Buddhas were masters of the inner work that they have been the best, the most powerful influence for the perfection of the outer life of mankind.

Finally, we have urged each one to undertake this inner work that, by its spiritual force, will bring harmony and peace to the necessary activities of the individual and society, and the Divine Life to mankind on earth and in the eternal.

Thus it was that Christ said, "It is not I, but the Father within me, Who doeth the work." Then can we say with the Psalmist: "May the beauty of the Lord be upon us and establish thou the work of our hands; yea, the work of our hands, establish thou it."[23]

THE PROBLEM OF FREE WILL

Chapter XVII

A RECONCILIATION OF
CONTRARIES

––––––

The question of whether the omnipotence of God and the free will of man are incompatible is one of the most ancient and esoteric religious and philosophical problems. If they are compatible, is this a paradox? How can it be that the Divine sees and directs all, yet man at the same time enjoys independent freedom of choice? If man is free, the argument runs, God is not all-powerful; if God is all-powerful, man is not free.

There are some religions that possess exactly opposite views on this question and rank it as a salient theological issue. Let us cite a few instances that are familiar to us in our own country. The Presbyterian church in its early years subscribed to a form of predestination as put forth by John Calvin. The Free Will Baptists, who call themselves by that name, believe completely in man's free will, and not in God's predestination. Most Baptists are not in agreement with this. The primitive Baptists, on the other hand, believe entirely in God's predestination and not in man's free will. These opposite views, to which each of these particular Baptist sects is devoutly and earnestly committed, affect their religious attitudes and their organizational practices.

Because of their belief in God's predestination, the primitive Baptists do no missionary work such as other denominations perform. In Asia there is a variant of predestination, known as karma. This is a belief that a person's past lives determine what their present life will be. Involved here are such questions as whether the exertion of will is of any effect at all, and whether God has foreknowledge of events. Yet it is unnecessary to take one side of this issue and reject the other, or to favor one of these sincerely held religious convictions over the other. These are not contraries, this is not an enigma; these opposing views can be reconciled.

Divine omnipotence and human free will are neither incompatible nor paradoxical. That there seems to be a conflict between them is due to the limitations of human reason. What seems to be contradiction and paradox to the human mind is harmonized in a higher knowledge. As has been said, in God all things find their secret reconciliation.

The question might be asked, Why does an omnipotent God

permit satanic or hostile forces at all, to beleaguer the human race with temptation and evil? The reply is that these hostile attacks spur man on to perfect himself, to overcome his impurity and weakness, and thus to immunize himself against such attacks. Thus the hostile agencies become divine energies which, behind a mask, aid in the self-transformation of the individual. They are, in a hidden way, collaborators in our divinization.

Chapter XVIII

THE PARTISAN MIND

Beneath all of this seeming hostility is the hand and joy of God, teaching, guiding, leading us to the Eternal. There is a proverb in which a wise man says: I have learned more from my enemies than I ever learned from my friends. Thus do we learn from all our teachers. All of us have had the experience of profiting from mistakes which we correct, and gaining from misfortunes which we surmount. This means that we learn in certain ways, but it does not signify that we are not free in our will.

What quality of the human reason would cause it to deem that God's power and man's free will are incompatible? It is this: Man's mind, as now constituted, is prone to grasp only partial or special truths and to cling to them rather than to discover the full truth and adhere to it. The mind is inclined to be partisan. It is usually unable to see the elements of truth in all religions, philosophies, and science, and to reconcile them, instead of adopting one to the exclusion of the others. It becomes a fierce disputant or champion of one or the other, and embroils man in quarrels over their relative merit and claims. It is apt to accept one religious belief or scientific hypothesis, and to discount or discredit all others. It does the same with respect to economic theories, healing arts, and so many other belief systems.

This is at once the limitation and the virtue of human reason. Its close pursuit of one path leads to a skillful grasp of its particular field. At the same time this narrowness cuts it off from unitary truth in nature, let alone the higher truth beyond nature, into which it is not competent to venture at all.

Let us consider another example. This one is in the social field, the vital issue of civil rights now before the American people. There are two positions here: One is that more and stronger civil rights legislations should be enacted. That is true, and it is generally conceded that such laws will soon be passed. Such is the truth in this position.

The other position is that legislation cannot force mankind to accord true equality to its fellows, that laws cannot force us to love one another. This view holds that true equality will transpire only when mankind's nature is so transformed that through its own free will and voluntary action it will in its heart and soul cease to discriminate or be prejudiced against its fellow kind for any reason whatsoever. This second position is also true.

Yet these two outlooks are not incompatible, no matter how earnestly the adherents of each side may be convinced of the exclusive rightness of their respective doctrines. The solution is in recognizing the element of truth in both positions. Stronger civil rights laws must be adopted as necessary until mankind's evident love for its kind can make the compulsion of law in such matters a given for an orderly and peaceful society. The soul will then do voluntarily, gladly, and in full what the statute books must otherwise and meanwhile do as best they can. Then the will of the spirit in man will not suffer any other individual to be deprived of equality before the law or before God. Thus the free will of humanity in time becomes the free will of the Spirit of God which Paul said dwells within him.

Chapter XIX

EGOISTIC FREE WILL

———

What is the difference between these two kinds of free will? The first is egoistic free will and the second is psychic free will or the free will of the soul. We shall first define these two kinds of will, and next consider how to rise from the first to the second, from the lower to the higher motivation, from the egocentric to the cosmic.

Egoistic free will is a product of the determinism of nature. While it is the lesser form of free will, it still has an indispensable and valuable role in an individual's development. The determinism of nature is the environment in which an individual lives and is a part of. This determinism of nature is what strongly influences the decisions one makes in their development of the egoistic free will.

I think that I make certain decisions of my own free and independent choice, but actually in that choice I am influenced by a host of factors. My surroundings, my past and present conditions; my heredity, history, and present context all exert their pulls upon me and influence my personal development. Then there are the pressures of family, religion, politics, customs, and communal or geographical prejudices or preferences. All of these I consciously or subconsciously weigh when reaching my decision.

Thus my egoistic free will is not altogether a free agent. Nevertheless, it is an advance in my evolution. Initially a choice is made and a free will is exercised, even if influenced by the conditions and ignorance of nature and by the ignorance of our own mind which itself is a part of nature. Human beings alone have taken this step toward a free self.

The animal has no ego from which to rise. The animal has neither the problems nor the potentialities of the ego. The animal is unaware of any free self within, as humans are. It is through this inner free self that we have already shaken off the yoke of nature and become its master in many respects. The egoistic free will is thus a step forward. It will lead to a greater potentiality, a purer and higher free will, a greater mastery over ourselves and nature than we have yet achieved.

Considerable good has resulted from egoistic free will, and also much that is bad, because of its mixed and impure nature.

On the positive side, mankind's natural environment has ingrained in our minds ideals of orderly, industrious, ethical behavior and other virtues. On the other hand, if one's surrounding influences are regressive, the opposite of good ideals may be implanted, so long as such a regime exists. Thus in one society communal pressure may encourage the egoistic free will to be liberty loving, tolerant, and law abiding; and in another it may force or sway an individual to give allegiance to a regime which stands for the opposite. It may make a person the puppet of a totalitarian, autocratic, unjust government. In a toxic environment, an individual may learn to look complacently and unresistingly upon the casting aside of every liberty of conscience and common decency for which humanity has labored through the ages.

Chapter XX

PSYCHIC FREE WILL

———

In summary, egoistic free will responds to the determinism of nature. It is largely shaped by the ignorance, errors, and confusion that are still encountered in the natural world as each individual makes their way forward and upward beyond the solitary self.

We reach now the second kind of free will: free will of the soul or psyche. It is this that takes mankind beyond the limitation of egoistic free will. The egoistic free will is not wrong in believing that there is free will. It does exercise choice, even if it is a choice determined principally by nature. It errs only in believing that it is the center of our action, and that all exists because of it. The ego is not wrong in thinking that there is a person within us who acts freely and for whom all exists, but the ego is wrong in thinking that it is that person. The free person is the spirit of God within us—the soul. Where egoistic free will acts in ignorance, limited by finite nature, the soul acts in knowledge in the limitless light of the Divine. Where egoistic free will is perturbed, is at a loss for what to decide, and decides often with costly error, psychic free will is calm, foresees all, and acts unerringly.

When we progress to the point where the psychic free will becomes preeminent in the governance of our being, the domination and missteps of egoistic free will vanish from us. This does not mean that we cease to act. It means that our actions have greater possibilities, even to the infinite ranges of glory. Present human activities and achievements will then be but a shadow compared with what is to unfold in the future.

What mankind has achieved through egoistic free will has been remarkable, albeit far from perfect; yet that achievement will be infinitesimal compared to the grandeur and near perfection of the attainments that the psychic free will is to bring to pass for mankind. As the Bible says, eye has not seen and ear has not heard, neither has it entered the heart of man the things which God has prepared for them that love Him. Even science declares that the possibilities for the future lie beyond our present scope of knowledge.

This change, as has been said, is the evolution of the nature and the consummation of the Divine birth. "When it is accomplished, the Soul is aware of itself as the master of its nature and, grown a light of the Divine Light and will of the Divine Will, is able to change its natural workings into a Divine action."[24]

It is said in the Talmud: "Everything is foreseen, yet freedom of choice is given: and the world is judged by grace, yet all is according to the amount of the work."[25]

As the mother who watches unceasingly over her infant child knows that the child must learn to be free and independent, so the Divine watches solicitously and tenderly over us, as we grow to realize our freedom in the liberty of God. What the Divine predestines to glory, he justifies in freedom.

So spoke the Apostle Paul in his letter to the Romans: "We know that all things work together for good to those who love God, to those who are called according to His purpose. For whom He foreknew, He also predestined to be conformed to the image of His son, that he might be the firstborn among many brethren. Moreover whom He predestined, these He also called; whom He called, these He also justified; and whom He justified, these He also glorified."[26]

SACRIFICE

Chapter XXI

THE SELF-CONSCIOUS
BEING OF MAN

———

One cannot become spiritual without sacrifice. It is impossible to attain spiritual realization without it. This is confirmed by observation of various activities below the spiritual plane.

Does not the musical virtuoso spend endless hours in study and practice for the perfection of her art? Does she not sacrifice her time, energy, and efforts on the altar of her artistic muse, so that she can evoke beauty for mankind? Is not the same true of the scientist who throws himself entirely against the forces of nature to discover its secrets, so that he can harness energies for the utilitarian benefits of mankind? Is it not true, even on the mere physical plane, with the athlete who must spend hours conditioning and preparing for the contest of strength and stamina? All of this is true, and even more so in the spiritual endeavor, so that you can be one with God. You have to learn its training rules and disciplines and observe them rigorously; you have to devote the necessary time; and finally you must avoid all that diverts your attention to other objects, or saps your energy and causes you to falter or fail in your sublime aim.

I was asked recently, Is not sacrifice a misnomer? I replied that it is not; it is a fundamental principle of all existence. Its highest practice is an interchange between the individual soul and the Divine. But there is another element which should be added.

Mankind has what might be called an independent role in making this sacrifice. We are the only self-conscious being that Nature has evolved. We are the only species of life that is born unfinished and required to finish our own development. This is true in every plane of existence: physiologically, psychologically, and spiritually. We are free to rise to the height of the gods or sink to the lowest depths of the forces of evil. Mankind is endowed with the unique gift of freedom. Unlike other life, we are beings who have conscious minds and wills that are not completely dominated by nature, as are the animals.

We are not merely creatures of circumstance; at any moment we can choose to transcend all circumstance and begin a new life. We have the power of self-transcendence. We possess an increasing capacity of self-determination and self-development as well as an independent part in shaping our own evolutionary progress.

The divine arrangement is such that man's free consent is required for the sacrifice made to God. This is not because the Divine is unable to compel a person to participate in the interchange between soul and God; it is because freedom is the primary principle of the spiritual, as it is in the mundane or earthly. Freedom is the rule of God's dealings with the self-conscious beings we are. The Divine does not force His will on us; He does not compel us to aspire to Him, to sacrifice or to dedicate ourselves to Him.

Mankind, the self-conscious being, is left free to do this or not to do this. Our sacrifice, like our submission to God, has to be willing and voluntary.

Chapter XXII

THE TRANSFORMATIVE SACRIFICE
OF INNER PURIFICATION

————

There are three additional points on sacrifice: the nature of our sacrifice, the purpose of our sacrifice, and last, the rules of sacrifice.

As to the nature of sacrifice, most people think of sacrifice as an external offering of some kind; but actually all our movements, our internal actions no less than our outward deeds, must be placed upon the one altar. If our purpose were merely to escape to some nirvanic plane of existence or to a distant paradise beyond the world, then we might not be concerned with reconciling the external sacrifice with the internal sacrifice. We might simply renounce external and material things and withdraw from the world. This, or some phases of it, at times may be necessary, but it is not the highest sacrifice. The great sacrifice is the inner offering of yourself to the Divine. We do this not as an escape from life, but in order that by purifying and transforming ourselves inwardly, we may bring a purification and transformation to the life of humanity and of the world.

This is the nature of our sacrifice, and one that we should always have before us. If we are in constant remembrance of this, then we will not be haunted by the idea that we can become spiritually acceptable merely by external renouncements. Nor, on the other hand, will we be deluded into believing that we can shut ourselves up into a shell of isolation and leave our peers and the world behind in ignorance and darkness.

In the life of every great spiritual teacher and prophet there has always been this dual sacrifice. First, any external sacrifice that seems required, even unto death, as it came to Christ will be made. Second, the supreme inner sacrifice of oneself to the Divine Truth is made in order to share it with others for their liberation. It should be understood, however, that a tragic fate is not inevitable and becomes less and less likely for the spiritual teachers of mankind. Buddha, Moses, Mohammed, and Confucius all lived out their full life spans amid honor and recognition. The case of Christ happened to be complicated by the presence of the armies of a foreign conqueror, the Roman Empire, which viewed Christ through the suspicion of insurrection, and put him to death. This peculiar circumstance did not exist in relation to the other four examples mentioned.

The second point is the purpose of our sacrifice. This is to illumine all our inner movements as well as our external doings. It is to effect a transformation of the motive force of our lives and the character of all our works. We are to abandon all lesser values and superficial good. We are to turn from all other calls and take refuge in God alone. Such a severe and drastic change in the direction and motive of our actions compels a corresponding Divine response. This brings down a Higher Consciousness into every movement and plane of our being and purifies them. The Soul then comes forward and imposes Its will upon all of our outer members. The mind becomes quiet and no longer sustains itself in every particular, on the sufficiency of its mental ideas. The emotions are steadied and controlled and no longer rashly or crudely insist on their cravings and desires. The physical, too, is changed so that it does not snuff out the inner flame under the heaviness, obscurity, and inertia of its outer mass.

The sense of sacrifice effects a subtle, all-pervasive change in us. It enables our inmost psychic being to come forward, which otherwise is but rarely evident in our lives. This gives us a one-pointed orientation toward the Divine with a plasticity and sureness that leads us directly to the truth. He in whom this sacrifice is strong automatically distinguishes the right from the wrong, and can separate the undivine alloys from the divine and Godward aspiration.

It can thus be seen how sacrifice will alter our entire existence. It will cause us to insist on truth, on will and strength and mastery, on joy and love and beauty, and a truth of abiding knowledge. It does so not for mere individual pleasure but for the divinization of our life and the lives of all, the expression of a higher truth, and of dedication to the Divine and Eternal.

Chapter XXIII

REJECTION OF THE EGO &
PRIORITIZATION OF THE SOUL

———

Individuals who have made this sacrifice become transformed even in their appearance. One can feel in them that ego has vanished. The Soul appears in their very eyes; it can be seen in the expression of their faces, heard in the sound of their voices. These seekers are guided unerringly to the truth in all events and circumstances. They are no longer sunk in a quagmire of doubt, humiliation, and agonizing self-appraisal as to what their conduct should be and the nature of their reactions in individual and social existence.

Many people would like to be thus free and unfettered, joyous and full of light; but until they learn to offer the sacrifice of themselves and know why they are offering it, they cannot achieve this liberation. This is the essence of the interchange which you undertake on your part, by your own free choice. A sacrificial offering is not a sacrifice unless you bring it to the altar yourself. You cannot entrust it to some ecclesiastical officer or priestly functionary, it must ascend from your inmost being to the highest sanctuary of God.

Let us now turn to the third and last point, which are the rules of our sacrifice. There are two principal rules which, if followed, will lessen the difficulties and dangers that often face those who sincerely attempt this sacrifice. First, one must reject all that comes from the ego. Second, one must accept all that comes from the soul. To reject what comes from the ego means to put aside the presumptuous incompetence of ideas, and driving impulses of passion, all that pushes us into the arms of ignorance. To hear and follow the voice of the soul requires that we heed the direction of spiritual teachers and spiritual laws and principles that help us to be master of ourselves so that we may become our own sure guides under the Supreme Divine Knowledge.

If we cannot give up these egoistic weaknesses, or think in our mental ignorance that we can rely on our personal mind alone, unillumined by a higher knowledge, we cannot hope to discover the way to the true inner law. Instead, we only build up self-created obstacles that impede our divine fulfillment. However, if you are able to recognize and renounce these obscuring and impeding agencies, if you can learn to recognize and follow the true spiritual guide, both within and without, you will discover the spiritual law and the goal of spiritual realization.

This complete change of your consciousness achieved by progressive stages and increasing volume is the entire meaning and also the method of the spiritual quest for union with God.

Three points have been outlined: the Nature, the Purpose, and the Rules of sacrifice. From these observations, we should be able to gain an ever-increasing realization as to why sacrifice is central to all spiritual endeavor. It is the very central theme of Christianity, the sacrifice of Christ. In every other religion it is the same. Even in nonreligious countries it is the same. In countries today which wrongly forbid the practice of religion, the idea of sacrifice is still the strongest subjective theme of the national existence, but is distorted to be as devoted to the interests of a certain class or a certain race, as has occurred in Russia and Germany. Here the individual is asked to sacrifice himself and all that he is and does, not to the Divine, but to the external machine of the State, or to certain ancestry. It is not a question of doing without sacrifice; that will never come. It is what you sacrifice for and to whom and how. When the individual learns this lesson of sacrifice, she will have discovered the path to the Immortal.

LIBERATION FROM GUILT

Chapter XXIV

WHAT IS GUILT?

————

Guilt is a legal term which has been introduced into the lexicon of various religions. It may have its origin in some long-vanished era when our more primitive selves felt forced to rely more upon the threat of punishment as the best inducement to follow the good life. However that may be, due to certain religious teachings of sin, guilt, and punishment, numerous people go through life with guilt feelings hanging over them because of what they consider to be their past mistakes, or those of mankind in general. Even when they have mentally ceased to believe in the theology of guilt and punishment, it has been so psychologically ingrained in them that only with much difficulty can they shake off the haunting memory of past remorses . . . the—I should have done this/I should not have done that—guilt feelings of old or recent unnecessary self-reproaches.

If past mistakes or errors are not sin, what are they? This question may be answered from the background of individual experience and that of collective human existence. Each of us can look back upon our lives and pick out errors or mistakes. Why were they committed? It might have been because of youthful inexperience; or perhaps we had not gained the best set of values, or an adequate knowledge in our early environmental surroundings, whether those of home, school, associates; or there might have been a lack of education or absence of thorough spiritual training.

The mistakes were made, for any one of a number of reasons, because we, as individuals, did not know enough to avoid making them. I can confess that I have made mistakes for the reasons I have enumerated, as others have likewise. If the conditions had been reversed and the individual had possessed the advantage of better training and education and the right spiritual motivation, the errors by and large might not have occurred at all, or at a much lesser degree, and more infrequently.

At a later age we set out to gain the kind of associates, the scope of knowledge, and the kind of spiritual experience which we then realize would more nearly have guided us rightly in the first place. Again, I am not speaking theoretically, since I have gone through this process myself. I had to realize that I was a conglomeration of misunderstandings and half-developed comprehension, and prone to the errors which these cause, before I could make a start toward knowledge.

Are we guilty because we did not have the right motivation and advantages in the first place? Not at all. They were not present in our consciousness; we were ignorant of their existence and unable to trespass deliberately against something of which we had no knowledge. It is for this reason that the Bible says that he who knows and does not do, sins. The converse is true. He who does not know does not sin, but is ignorant of his offenses. Yet there is an escape, for if ignorance is the cause of error, we are moving out of ignorance toward knowledge and perfection. So what awaits mankind is not condemnation and punishment, but liberation and perfection.

Chapter XXV

THE IMMORALITY
OF THEOLOGICAL GUILT

I am not advocating the removal of guilt and punishment from the penal codes of society. Guilt and punishment are processes that governments are now compelled to use. They must continue to use them until human ignorance disappears. The law will go on invoking penalties upon errant individuals until the soul becomes the ruler of life and society, for in the spirit men do not err, and their governments will be of a higher order.

Guilt has no place at all in the spiritual. There are world religions such as Buddhism in which there are no such things as sin and guilt. But some religions attempt to apply theological guilt not only to individuals, but also to whole groups, classes, and races. This, likewise, has no true basis. In such cases, categories of people are depicted as theologically guilty because they belong to a certain class, or their skin is of a certain color, or for other reasons no more valid.

For instance, there are in this country today some religious beliefs that teach, according to the Bible, that God is a segregationist and that other races are the result of some ancient sin of which one of its members is guilty and can never in eternity have a spiritual status equal to that of the white race. There are no such teachings in the Bible.

The point here is that theological guilt has been laid, not upon a single individual, but upon a whole race comprising hundreds of millions of people, and inhabiting one of the major continents of the globe, living in many other countries, in large numbers, including our own country. There is, however, a rising protest among religious sects against this kind of racial discrimination. Many of their leaders have been in the forefront of movements to eliminate such prejudices, in accordance with the words of Apostle Paul that God made of one blood all nations of men.

If you have suffered individual guilt feelings from such inner disturbances as hate, jealousy, or envy, you can easily imagine the suffering of a whole class or race of people upon whom is placed the gratuitous stigma of guilt and inferiority, both in heaven and on earth, which in no way applies to them.

Chapter XXVI

REMOVING THEOLOGICAL GUILT

There are signs that this kind of theological guilt attributed to masses of people in Western religion is beginning to yield to pressure against it from within the ranks of the religions themselves, both in our country and elsewhere. For instance, in 1964 the Ecumenical Council held in Rome by the Catholic Church published a document declaring that there was no Biblical basis for the hatred or persecution of the Jewish people because of the crucifixion of Christ. The document declares that it is unjust to call the Jewish people God killers or accursed by God, since all men are responsible for the crucifixion and bear the guilt for it, and that the guilt cannot be charged to the whole Jewish people of the time of Christ or today.

It is utter nonsense to affix guilt and curses upon the Jewish people because of the crucifixion, for all the reasons now given by the Catholics and many others. This conciliatory step by the Catholics (to reconcile Christianity and Judaism), though nearly 2,000 years overdue, is the welcome sign of an encouraging tendency. But let us note that while it removes the stigma of theological guilt from the Jewish people in the matter, it lays the guilt upon all mankind.

It is fitting and proper that this theological guilt is being removed from the Jewish people, but it would be better if it were removed from all men, Jews and non-Jews alike; for just as it has now been realized that the Jewish people have no guilt for the crucifixion of Christ, it will inevitably be realized that neither does mankind as a whole. Theological guilt is a passing religious dogma, and not an eternal spiritual truth. As it is going out, in the case of the Jewish people in particular, so it will cease with respect to mankind in general.

This conception of guilt has not only separated the Jewish people from the Christians in the past, but today separates Christianity from the rest of mankind, who do not regard themselves as born inheritors of a sectarian guilt. The Catholic Church originally applied such a guilt concept to the Muslims as well as the Jewish people. Pope Innocent the Third told the Fourth Lateran

Council in the year 1215 that the Jewish people were eternally condemned to servitude. The Council ruled that Jews and Muslims, of both sexes in every Christian province, would be marked off in the eyes of the public from other people through the character of their dress. The decree required that Jews and Muslims from the age of twelve and upward wear distinctive badges of yellow cloth sewn to their clothing. Thus, not only the Jews, but the Muslims were placed under a theological guilt. The infamous decree of the Nazis during World War II requiring Jews to wear distinctive yellow badges, therefore, had a theological origin more than 700 years old. From this can be observed some of the terrible havoc of the guilt doctrine on religion.

The ill effects of guilt theology are obvious in both individual and social life. It has already been shown that within individuals it creates an internal war and deep self-inflicted psychological wounds. Guilt or inferiority wrongly stamped upon the group psychology of vast numbers of people belonging to certain races, religions, or other classes causes social unrest, bitterness, violence, and war.

It should be noted that the guilt concept is not held by the Catholics alone, but has been a main doctrine of Christian theology in general. It arises from the theological belief that the human race is guilty of original sin, and can be saved from that guilt only by the atonement of Christ on the cross; but here, also, there are protests. One of the largest Christian denominations has denied the proposition of original sin or the possibility of eternal damnation, which I have mentioned, and there are others as well. All the religions have their glories, and also some chapters in their past which are not so glorious, and from which they have to advance, and many of them have done so.

Chapter XXVII

REMOVING PERSONAL GUILT:
FROM IGNORANCE TO KNOWLEDGE

———

Let us now turn to the question of how to rid ourselves of guilt feelings. First, we should have the clear understanding that not guilt but ignorance is the problem. To get rid of the guilt idea, especially the mental idea of theological guilt, is not too difficult. All this requires is a change in your thoughts, the discarding of a mental concept or theory.

To eradicate guilt feelings that have been ingrained is much more difficult. To do so requires transformation of the entire being: mental, emotional, and physical. I can correct a thought more easily than I can transform my entire self. Individuals often act contrarily to what their thoughts tell them is best.

Perhaps it is easier to plead guilt and ask forgiveness than it is to admit ignorance and seek knowledge; but we are seeking to move from ignorance to knowledge. It is only those who know they are ignorant who can advance to knowledge. The more ignorant a person is the less he is willing to admit it.

Two opposite personalities struggle within us for control in this movement from ignorance to knowledge. One resists the change. This personality is largely emotional and physical. It urges you to continue to be the old self that you have been. This person impels you over and over again to recommit the same stupidities and blunders that you are trying to overcome. If, for instance, you have been prone to angry outbursts and irritation, the old flare-ups will occur again at the least provocation. This person in you is like a volcano that is sometimes dormant but will unpredictably erupt, spilling hot and searing lava, spewing smoke and fire, and leaving behind ashes of remorse.

But there is another person who is calling for the change, and insists upon it. This is your psychic being, the Soul. It seeks to bring about a new birth in you. For this it endeavors to bring the struggle from the outer emotional and physical planes where you are the weakest to the psychological and inner. If you can do this your progress will be faster and surer. Time will be required, but if you begin to get control over your actions, control over your thoughts and feelings is certain to follow.

If you can cease to act in anger, soon you will no longer think or feel anger. As the Bible says, "Be angry but do not sin; do not let the sun go down on your anger, and do not make room for the devil."[27] This means that if you do happen to get angry, you should not allow it to cause you to do wrong, and you should not prolong the anger. The devil referred to here is that person in you who is pulling you in the wrong direction.

The suggestions and promptings of the old self, the resisting personality, should always be denied. If you give way to it, you give it a new hold and opportunity to strike again, but if you always heed your psychic being through prayer and aspiration to the Divine, you will receive the right ideas and impulses that will make possible the transformation of your nature.

If you do this you will succeed, despite all temporary lapses. Lapses and backslides are sometimes for the purpose of calling attention to weaknesses in you that need correction. You should proceed quietly to correct them and avoid any nervous or inner wringing of hands. All such excitements only invite attacks of the lower forces. If you are not overwrought, but calm, you can bring to bear an intent but quiet observation through which you watch for the defects and weed them out.

You can learn to look upon your backslides with a smile, as things that may persist intermittently for a while because of habit, but that will go away in the end. You will see the absurdity of doing things that hurt your health and slow your spiritual progress. These things will become to you not only injurious but ridiculous. A sense of humor is an aid to the spiritual devotee.

As Sri Aurobindo says, this is a spiritual battle; to attempt it is to stir up all kinds of adverse forces, and you must be prepared to face difficulties, sufferings, and reverses of all kinds in a calm, unflinching spirit.[28]

These difficulties that are met are ordeals and tests, and if one meets them in the right way, they become aids to our progress; one comes out stronger and spiritually purer and greater. No matter what misfortune may occur, the adverse forces cannot hamper us unless there is some defect in ourselves, some weakness, impurity, or ignorance. This weakness we should then seek out and eliminate.

What is the role of forgiveness if it is not guilt, but ignorance, that is the difficulty? Forgiveness is a patient forbearance which recognizes that the individual has weaknesses to overcome and that this takes time. Christ would say to the fallen, "Your sins are forgiven, go and sin no more." As to how many times we should forgive, he said, "seventy times seven." He knew that it is a struggle for men to overcome the weaknesses common to them all, but that the way is provided for those to do so who have the divine aspiration. As the Apostle Paul wrote to the Corinthians: "No temptation has overcome you that is not common to everyone. God is faithful, and He will not let you be tested beyond your strength, but with the testing will also provide the way out so that you may be able to endure it."[29]

FORGIVENESS

Chapter XXVIII

UNDERSTANDING FORGIVENESS

Among the religions there are differing theological concepts concerning forgiveness, and a widely felt need for it among people. In order to gain an idea of the importance attached to it in religion, let us first consider the place of forgiveness as a relationship between God and the individual in Judaism, Christianity, and Buddhism, as examples.

In Judaism the holiest day of the year is Yom Kippur, the Day of Atonement. This is a day of fasting and repentance, of asking God for pardon of transgressions. The great prayer, the Kol Nidre, is sung on that day. In it the cantor asks God to forgive past transgressions, but also all resolves and vows which the people may make and not be able to keep in the year to come.

We repent them all, says the cantor of these vows, May they be held by the Almighty to be of no moment.

This is a prior admission that despite all their solemn resolves not to transgress again, the people will do so, and therefore they ask forgiveness from God in advance.

The congregation answers, And pardon shall be granted to the whole congregation of Israel, and to the stranger who sojourns among them, when all the people transgress ignorantly.

We may observe that Judaism is correct in attributing transgression to ignorance, but we hope in this discussion to revise its concept of the inevitability of transgression in order to show that man may rise above all transgression and impurity.

It is no discredit to Judaism that we make this amendment, for its own great rabbis believe that spiritual knowledge advances and they have correctly seen that transgression springs from ignorance.

In Christian theology the central theme is the sacrifice of God's son, Christ, upon the cross to obtain forgiveness for the sins of mankind; the life of Christ is offered to God as an expiation for human transgressions. Whoever believes this and accepts Christ as such a sacrifice, his sins are forgiven and he receives eternal life and bliss in heaven; whoever rejects this belief has no forgiveness and no salvation in this world or the world to come.

The fundamental Christians express it this way: You must be covered by the Blood of the Lamb to be saved, the Lamb being Christ sacrificed on the altar to God. This, to many, has overtones of animal sacrifice practiced in religious rites long before Christ lived, and of which we read in the Bible. The sacrifice of the animal was a substitute offering for one's sins, the life of the animal being taken instead of one's own life for one's sins. Hence rises the saying regarding Christ, that our sins were laid on Him.

This sacrifice theology is not peculiar to the Jews; it is found in many other religions from the earliest times. Buddha sought to stop it in India. Once he saw a herd of sheep being led from the beautiful pastures on the green hills to the temple, to be slaughtered as a sacrifice to the gods by the priests. Buddha followed the sheep into the temple and said gently to the priest and the people, "You cannot lay your sins on the heads of these innocent beasts." Buddha turned the sheep loose and they returned to their green pastures. Such was Buddha's piety and gentleness that the priest and people stood silent, and no one interfered or sought to stop him.

Even these more primitive or undeveloped concepts of sacrifice and forgiveness have concealed within them a larger truth. This is to be disclosed by the increasing spiritual consciousness of mankind, as it rises from ignorance toward increasing spiritual consciousness and then toward a divine knowledge. It is this larger truth of forgiveness that we shall discuss. We shall see that it was for this more profound reason that Christ really sacrificed his life. As we no longer lay animals on the altar for sacrifice, neither need we any longer consider Christ a substitute sacrifice, but a Divine Incarnation, showing us, as he did, the path to peace and eternal life. We do not lay our sins on Christ, but our hopes for glory and the immortal.

Chapter XXIX

FORGIVENESS FROM THE HEART

———

Next, let us turn our attention to the deep individual concern about forgiveness. A need for forgiving and being forgiven stirs deeply within people and seeks a proper outlet. Religions, cognizant of the problem, have attempted to provide such an outlet or solution. Ministering as they do to multitudes of people, religions in the main have been obliged to fall back on external forms of exculpation. They have done so not because these ceremonies were the best or the highest, but because they were almost the only means available or suitable for large numbers of people at the present stage of human development.

These ceremonial forms are far advanced over the practices

of animal sacrifice. They had to be made suitable to the greatest majority of people, and often this was accomplished with striking beauty and effect in scripture, prayer, liturgy, and sacred music.

Thus it is that in many religions individuals seek forgiveness for themselves or for others by standard external rites and observances. Among them are confession to priests, repeated recitation of certain prayers, charity, priestly indulgences, and many others.

There are also outmoded extremes, such as self-mortification. I have heard of a lingering example of this in our own Southwest, in the practices of the Penitentes of New Mexico, who put themselves to blood-letting self-punishment at Easter. Yet even such violent forms of penance are evidence that mankind is conscious of evil and error, and determined in the best way to make recompense for and overcome it. The ways in which humanity seeks to do this have become more and more elevated and gentle, and less obscure and barbarous as our spiritual wisdom has progressed.

God looks with understanding and justice on any sincere penitent, and the most simple penance and a better view of penance occurs in man as he advances toward a higher light and a divine existence. There is a dawn and a high noon in the forgiveness principle, and mankind is moving toward the brighter light.

Physical self-mortification for the sake of forgiveness has largely ceased in civilized nations, but the same cannot be said for psychological self-mortification. Many highly civilized people suffer psychologically from a need for forgiveness. This is as useless and anachronistic as physical self-flagellation. It no more belongs to our day than the bodily mortification of ancient religious zealots who flogged themselves with spiked iron whips until the blood ran. Yet many people still suffer from inner remorse for past mistakes, and need help to overcome it.

It is as bad and harmful to mortify the mind and the emotions as it is to disfigure the body for penitential reasons. A proper understanding of what true forgiveness is, and confidence in the Divine, will enable one to overcome this unhappy self-reproach.

Forgiveness too often implies guilt. We seem to have done wrong and feel guilt. To cleanse ourselves of the guilt we do penance, but guilt is not the essence of forgiveness. If Christ had felt that guilt was the essence, he would not have said that you should forgive your brother seventy times seven times, and that it must come from the heart.

Chapter XXX

THE DANGERS OF IGNORANCE

———

Modern psychology emphasizes the damage and danger of guilt feelings. Religion bears some share of responsibility for this. It has at once assuaged the guilt feelings of mankind, yet has also perpetuated them.

Theological Christianity in the past, and still to a large extent in some quarters, has taught that man is guilty of original sin, and that he can win forgiveness for this, as we have said, only by believing that Christ died for him on the cross, as a sacrifice for man's sin.

Here a great truth has been diluted by later dogma. Christ did die for mankind, but not because we were guilty. He died that the false might become true; the bond, free; and the mortal become immortal. When he hung on the cross, Christ said of those who crucified him, "Forgive them, Father, for they know not what they do." Thus, Christ attributed what they did to ignorance—not guilt.

Ignorance crucified Christ, not any particular race, religion, or political power. It was not the Jews, Judaism, or the Roman Empire that crucified Christ, but ignorance.

So let us see if, like Christ, we can dissociate guilt and forgiveness.

The idea of theological guilt is a Western religious concept. It is not a belief subscribed to by all the world's great religions. It is not present in Confucianism, Buddhism, or Hinduism. In other words, it is not something endorsed by universal spiritual experience. Therefore, when we think we have done or said something for which we need forgiveness, and the matter is troubling us, let us abstain from the theologically imposed guilt feelings, and approach the problem from a different standpoint.

The first step in this new approach is to rid yourself of all feelings of inner guilt and unworthiness. It is not an approach of self-punishment, but self-understanding. As Sri Aurobindo said, "free yourself from all exaggerated self-deprecation and the habit of getting depressed by the sense of sin, difficulty, or failure."[30] These feelings do not really help; on the contrary, they are an immense obstacle, and hamper progress. They belong to the religious and not the spiritual mentality.

The spiritual seeker should look on all the defects of his nature as movements of the lower nature, common to all, and reject them calmly, firmly, and persistently, with full confidence in the Divine Power, without weakness or depression or negligence, and without excitement, impatience, or violence.

Even in modern criminology, the more advanced nations, laws, and courts consider that crimes are primarily due to psychological states of mind, and that proper treatment is more rehabilitative for the accused, and more beneficial to society, than the concept of guilt and punishment by itself.

Chapter XXXI

BECOMING A VESSEL FOR
DIVINE TRUTH

———

Often the harm that people do to themselves by worrying over a mistake is worse than the offense they may have committed against others, or think they have committed. This helps neither the other person nor the perpetrator. Worry is not the right inner attitude in regard to error. In answer to an inquiring disciple, Sri Aurobindo describes what the inner attitude and reparation should be, in these words:

"You ask how you can repair the wrong you seem to have done. Admitting that it is as you say, it seems to me that the reparation lies precisely in this, in making yourself a vessel for the Divine Truth and the Divine Love, and the first steps toward that are a complete self-consecration and self-purification, a complete opening of oneself to the Divine, rejecting all in oneself that can stand in the way of fulfillment. In the spiritual life there is no other reparation for any mistake, none other that is wholly effective. At the beginning one should not ask for any other fruit or results than this internal growth and change, for otherwise one lays oneself open to severe disappointments. Only when one is free can one free others, and in Yoga it is out of the inner victory that there comes the outer conquest."[31]

We see now why Christ said that forgiveness is from the heart. The wrong act for which we seek forgiveness is an outer manifestation of a life not divinely consecrated or purified within. It is this vessel of ourselves that has to be rededicated. This is the spiritual reparation; from it comes the outer victory over every fault or defect in ourselves.

Such an inner change has the power to melt away the grievance of those who are offended. They can see at a glance that all rancor has gone out of the offending person.

Aaron, the brother of Moses, was able to teach men how to dispel rancor. The Talmud calls him the Peace Maker, and relates this story:

Two men had fallen out and become enemies. Aaron went to one of them and told him how the other always spoke kindly and highly of him. The man began to weep and said to himself, Why have I offended that good man? Then Aaron went to the other man and told him the same thing, and he, too, began to weep and reproach himself for offending the other. The next time the two met they fell on each other's breast, kissed, and became friends again! Each saw that all rancor had departed from the other, and that inner forgiveness reigned in its place.

To be forgiving does not mean that others can wrong you with impunity, and without firm objection and successful resistance on your part. The forgiving are not arrogant, but they are not to be trampled upon.

The ancient rabbis said in the Talmud that a wise man is hard to anger, but not so sweet that he is consumed. You may forgive what is done in ignorance while using every just means to defeat it, and prevent its recurrence to harm or endanger yourself or the community.

God is the God of forgiveness, but of righteousness and power as well. He is forgiving, yet just; He loves, yet corrects; He sustains the good and crushes the evil, that all may come to light.

Chapter XXXII

THE STRONG FORGIVER IS
THUS PURIFIED

———

Christ had much to say about forgiveness; it was almost his last word on the cross. One of the most beautiful parables that he spoke was on this subject: the parable of the woman of the city who washed his feet with her tears, and dried them with her hair. "Therefore I tell you," said Christ, "her sins which are many are forgiven, for she loved much; but to whom little is forgiven, loves little ... your faith has saved you," said Christ to the woman, "go in peace."[32]

Christ meant by this parable that if our ignorance is little, we might not love God so much for helping us to dispel it; but when our ignorance is still so great as it is, when even Christ would not call himself good, when we are conscious of the throng of defects and weaknesses in us that we are steadily striving to cast out, how much and how great should be our love for God who teaches us to surmount such great darkness?

If God has shown us how to forgive and be forgiven, without lamentation or distress, but with joy and peace, shall we not love Him with an endless love? As portions of His Being, Souls of His All-Soul, let us be forgiving, merciful, and strong. The forgiver is not weak but strong; the strong individual is not vindictive, but merciful and forgiving.

In this discussion we have endeavored to remove from forgiveness all gloom, guilt, and misinterpretation. We see that these are found in lower forms of forgiveness that, however useful in earlier eras, are now outmoded and incompatible with the higher and developing consciousness of mankind.

We see, also, that external ceremonies of exculpation, though moving, beautiful, and helpful, are not the forgiveness in the heart, of which Christ spoke. We have shown that real forgiveness is a spiritual reparation in purity and calm. It sees ignorance, and not guilt, in the errors of mankind, even in the gravest, as Christ did.

We perceive that forgiveness is not an act by which our sins are expiated, but a sacrifice by which our lives are lifted to the Divine. Such is the sense in which Christ offered the sacrifice of himself on the cross for mankind. He was an instrument incarnate of the Divine Love, that all men might be like unto him. He died, not that we should be absolved of guilt, but inheritors of the Divine Sonship. We are not children of sin, but of God.

As John says in the New Testament, "Behold, now we are children of God; and it has not yet been revealed what we shall be, but we know that when He is revealed, we shall be like Him, for we shall see Him as He is. And everyone who has this hope in Him purifies himself, just as He is pure."[33]

LOVE

Chapter XXXIII

THE PERFECT & THE IMPERFECT

To be perfect is to be complete, entire, flawless in all that constitutes our existence. This is the goal of religions, philosophies, and science, how to live perfectly. In the Bible it is one of the injunctions of Jesus, "Be ye therefore perfect, even as your Father which is in Heaven is perfect."[34] We seek perfect salvation, perfect health, perfect joy, perfect security, and any diminution of these we deem an imperfection or misfortune.

Yet perfection is not understood, and the way to attain it is not known to most of us. To many people perfection seems to be a process of getting and not giving. If I can get this or that which I do not have, life will be perfect. If I had only done this and not the other, all would be perfect. This engenders a state of discontent. Such people, as Taoism teaches, spend their lives waiting for the future and seeking the past. They are disappointed, hurt, and frustrated at what life brings them. This, as Sri Aurobindo says, is the eternal fool in us. It is difficult for us to understand and accept that God the great workman is perfecting us by the blows he gives us, like the hammer blows on the anvil, like the fires that burn the dross out of the pure metal, the silver and gold. If there are psychological impurities within us, they must be removed before we can be refined, made perfect in knowledge, in emotions, in body. Therefore divine blows come to us on the psychological or subjective anvil until we are tempered. This is in order that we will not break or bend under the tasks and trials of life and in our progress toward liberation.

Perfection does not come by a demand on God but by a surrender to Him. In the silent communion within our breasts we realize that not our fallible thoughts but divine will is our guide to happiness and perfection. Then we become, as the Bible says, like little children; we have taken the first step toward perfection. You must make yourself as a little child to enter the Kingdom of God, said Jesus. This holy dependence is not slavishness. It is a principle of ordinary life necessary to life's fruitful functions. No one thinks of himself as a slave or an object if he follows some noble statesman politically, or in war if he fights to the end for a just cause by carrying out the orders of a heroic and resolute commander, nor do we brush aside the wise counsel of the leaders of civilian life. How much more, then, shall we look for spiritual perfection to the guidance and grace of Him who is the all-perfect, all-knowing, all-life, and all-power?

But we cannot have this at the point of a metaphysical gun. God is not mocked as the scriptures say and neither is he oblivious of what he knows is best for us, and that is what he brings to pass in our lives. Therefore the perfect person receives whatever comes their way from the divine without cavil. The perfect person has no selfish demands within. They have no hate to gloat over victims, no envy to subdue rivals, no greed to covet what belongs rightly to others, no egoism to crown themselves Lord, no ignorance that conceits them as the final source of wisdom on all subjects. They do not call their religion superior to that of others, for they would not harm others by destroying their faith but are content that God will lead all to ever-higher spiritual knowledge.

So let us take a new and different look at the question of perfection and imperfection. Let us see that perfection requires self-giving and self-understanding. It requires a realization of the meaning of existence. God did not make man or the world static. God is not only being but becoming. He is not only calm, detached, and passive, but energetic, involved, and active. The active aspect of the divine reality is the changing manifestation in the world, delighting in the labors of accomplishment and the overcoming of imperfections, the triumph of good over evil, of beauty over the sordid, of justice over injustice, of joy over sorrow, of freedom over subjection.

As children of God we must grow up spiritually, both as individuals and as a race, over the eras of progressing evolution. In all of this there is nothing wrong or unwise; on the contrary, there is joy if we feel the divine delight of the soul within us. For the soul is untouched by any vicissitude, and constantly impels our natural instruments of mind, emotions, and body toward ultimate perfection. He who has this delight is already immortal, for God is joy.

I am reminded here of a passage from the play *The Green Pastures*. God is shown in his office in Heaven during the time of Noah before the flood, when so much evil was among men on the earth. The Angels looking from Heaven at the earth said to Him, "Lord, there's so much trouble down on earth, why don't you just wipe it out and start all over?" "If you think that's trouble," answered the Lord, "you should have seen the trouble I had starting things up here." The wise man recognizes that this progression from imperfect to perfect is a reality from which he does not flinch or seek to withdraw, and seeing the beauty of God in all things, even those which seem repellant and ugly, he lives with joy and the certitude of knowledge.

I would like to make a practical application of the relationship of the perfect and imperfect to the field of personal problems. I am doing so because I often find that people who suffer emotional disturbances remain needlessly sick because of a misunderstanding of this subject. Perhaps we can follow the example of Buddha. When people came to him wanting to involve him in theological hair-splitting, he would not enter into such disputes. He would ask them—have you no problems? Isn't there anything wrong with you? Let's talk about that.

As an example of something that needs to be talked about, let us consider a common misunderstanding of perfection. I have had people approach me for counsel who were deeply disturbed. They were often sick and frantic with worry. Despair gripped them concerning health, finances, family problems. Some of these people whose distresses I endeavored to relieve, to the best of my ability and sympathy, would tell me that they were perfect, despite the obvious imperfection in their health and in their emotional, mental, and family life, since they were told so by their church and in their upbringing. So when it is intimated to them that they may have a misunderstanding of perfection they sometimes become offended or even insulted. If I ask if their sickness is a sign of perfect health they look at me in astonishment. If I ask them to glance about them and see if the world is perfect, they look at me in bewilderment and say they do not understand me.

So the first necessity in such cases is to state what perfection is in a more precise and accurate way. In their bewilderment such people sometimes cling to wrong movements within them such as egoism. They seem to expect the minister to sanction the causes of their sickness by affirming their perfection. The minister cannot help the sick or disturbed person in this way. This ignores and covers up weaknesses. Such concealed defects are left free to ravage the body while the individual continues to affirm the perfection of their imperfection.

The soul within us is perfect. But our outer nature, mind, life, and body, are far from perfect in most of us. Out of matter came life; out of life, mind appeared; beyond mind, the spirit is to become realized in our lives. This is the true course of evolution. The last stage, the emergence of the spiritual in life, will bring the advent of perfection that man in general has not yet attained. When that perfection is reached, there will proceed beyond it further and infinite perfections of which we cannot conceive, in which man shall pass as the Bible says from glory to glory. Now we aim to rise from imperfection to perfection. Then we shall rise from perfection to yet more glorious and ineffable perfection. For as the Bible says, "Eye hath not seen, nor ear heard, neither have entered into the heart of man, the things which God hath prepared for them that love him."[35] But it is necessary to be aware that mankind is generally at the stage of imperfection. Our species has highly developed its mental power but not its spiritual power. It is through the spiritual that perfection is realized.

At present we are faced with overcoming the ignorance of the mind, the storminess of the emotions, the sickness of the body. The perfect soul within us seeks to manifest itself by a corresponding perfection in all the exterior or bodily instruments. This is the real, the tremendous struggle now going on in the world. All social disturbance is really a reflection of this mighty subjective battle. Upon its outcome depends much more than individual healing. Without the victory of the spirit, mankind will not be victorious in harmonizing all that affects its outer and communal life.

To the extent that this perfection in the inner also becomes the perfection in the outer, we are able to conquer disease, to become masters of ourselves and of our environment, to understand the secrets of life, nature, and existence, to recognize our weaknesses and defects and how to overcome them, to remove not only our own distress but all that causes the miseries of the world in order to rise to the divine destiny of mankind.

Perfection is not simply a matter of affirmation, but transformation. I've read of one man who said that it took him eight years to discover what his faults were and to decide seriously to overcome them. It is a common saying in India that removing inner imperfections normally requires thirty-five years. Sincerity and total dedication can help the process move more quickly. But obviously no one can start the journey who does not first admit to himself that such a change has to be made, and recognize that he has imperfections to overcome. We have enough of a job to overcome our imperfections without handicapping ourselves by the delusion that they do not exist. At the same time we should realize that these failings are not peculiar to ourselves but are generally true of humanity and that with divine help all men shall rise above them to perfection.

Did Jesus call himself perfect? Was he perfectly good? Quite the contrary. He said, "Why do you call me good? No one is good but God alone."[36] Even when we experience communion with God we cannot stop with that high attainment. To be perfect spiritually we must then return and bring the divine perfection into mind, life, and body, in the individual and in the world.

This truth is well illustrated in the New Testament account of the transfiguration of Jesus. You might recall the three disciples, Peter, James, and John, ascended with him to the top of the mountain. There they experienced direct communion with God. Such was their ecstasy that Peter said, Lord, let us build tabernacles and stay here. But their request could not be granted for they had to return to suffering, diseased, and imperfect humanity. For perfection must be not only in heaven but on earth—not only in the soul but in the mind, in one's life activities, and body. The spirit is willing but the flesh is weak, says the Bible. That means not only the flesh of the individual but the flesh of the community—society, which has to be perfected also. This is the most difficult task of all, because matter is inert and difficult to change. This is integral perfection.

Total perfection in all planes, without perfection in any particular plane is impossible. It is so because the divine must be realized in the material as well as the spiritual, in life as well as beyond life, in the individual and also in the collectivity of humanity, and beyond in the transcendental. Here in this natural world God has manifested himself. When the poet Rabindra-nath Tagore asked, "What would God do without me," he meant that man is the visible expression of the divine reality under the conditions of nature. It is this expression that is still imperfect but is in the process of becoming perfect. We need not ask God's purpose in this because his purposes cannot be judged by human standards and terms. But it is leading mankind to unity, joy, free-dom, the immortal, and conscious union with God.

Ernest Holmes, founder of the Science of Mind movement, is quoted as saying that Jesus did not say that evil has no reality as an experience. In the same way it can be said that Jesus did not say imperfection has no reality as an experience. In fact, he spent much time pointing out imperfections in human nature and how to surmount them. He taught that life is more than food and the body more than raiment, and that he who finds his soul, his true being, would lose his imperfections. We should always distin-guish between the soul, which is our perfect eternal self, and the physical or external body, which is its natural instrument. It is by being preoccupied at all times with this outer self as the only reality, being constantly engrossed, clutching it tightly to our bosom, caressing it, that we become subject to its imperfections. But if we identify ourselves with the soul rather than exclusively with what happens to the body, then we are no longer torn apart by changing circumstances of outer life. We become masters of ourselves and our surroundings. In the soul we are joyous and serene and become thus in the body also. All desires to be great, powerful, superior, with their arrogance and egoism, leave us. We become truly humble and perfect in all things.

Unless this distinction between perfect and imperfect is understood, metaphysical teachings concerning perfection may inadvertently confuse some people and contribute to or establish their illnesses and distresses instead of healing and removing them.

Through this discussion we have endeavored to make such a distinction. We have tried to show how in the becoming process the imperfect can become perfect in every aspect of existence. We have not denied the obvious fact that imperfection now exists in us and in all men as a general thing. We have shown that by asking for and receiving divine aid and guidance, we can overcome these flaws. We should not undertake this task with feelings of weakness, fear, dejection, or guilt, but rather see that it is an evolving perfecting process by which we attain the divine life and the immortal. Jesus did not say, "You are perfect like your Father in Heaven." He did say, "Be ye perfect," that is, become perfect; let the outer self become as perfect as the inner soul within you in which is the Kingdom of God. The perfect and the divine within must be embodied in the external life of the individual and its culture in the natural world. Such is the object of the perfecting process, the key to the kingdom which Jesus said "is your Father's good pleasure to give unto you."[37]

Chapter XXXIV

PSYCHIC LOVE

The rabbinical scholars of the times of Jesus, who so far as we know were his only formal teachers, gave much emphasis to the question of how to study and learn. A section of a book of the Talmud is devoted to describing those who study closely with their teachers: "There are four qualities among those who study at the feet of teachers. They are like a sponge, a funnel, a sieve, and a sifter."[38] The sponge absorbs everything whether right or wrong. The funnel lets everything in at one end and out at the other, like the person of whom we say, whatever he hears goes in one ear and out the other. The sieve lets the good wine run through and keeps only the useless lees. But the sifter lets out the chaff and keeps the fine flour. So let us be sifters, separating the wheat from the chaff, keeping the fine flour of truth. Let us review and establish our knowledge on this subject and other vital matters as well. On this particular subject study and review are very essential, for a weak and sick body is an impediment to spiritual progress.

Some religionists, especially Christians, are prone to justify their illnesses by pointing to the passage in Second Corinthians 12:7 where Paul says he had a thorn in the flesh. They have interpreted this to mean that Paul suffered from a chronic illness of some kind. Scholars have speculated on what the nature of his illness was. Some say that his falling to the ground in a spiritual trance on the road to Damascus was really an epileptic attack.

An examination of the Aramaic or Eastern Text of the New Testament dispels this supposition. "Thorn in the flesh" was simply an Aramaic idiom of the time meaning trouble, annoyance, or worry. We use the same expression today without necessarily referring to illness at all. It is an idiom that has persisted through the centuries, and survived the changes from one language to another. Paul was referring to the attacks made on his work as an apostle by those who tried to keep the people from following him and who sought to discredit him in every way possible. Paul obviously was not a diseased man. No sick man could have withstood the beatings, stoning, shipwrecks, imprisonments, and rigorous land and sea journeys that he made. Paul was strong and the only infirmities he charged against himself were not weaknesses of the body but as an apostle in the spirit. This also was an Aramaic idiomatic expression of the day intended to show himself as truly humble.

Far from being weak and spiritless, Paul says, I have fought a good fight, I have finished my course, I have kept the faith. So let us, too, find the sources of healing power, in the soul, in the psyche, in the divine, so that we, too, like Paul, may become a good, strong, and healthy fighter. Let us not be weaklings, walked upon by every invading force, but strong as the great apostle to the Gentiles was strong.

Psychic love comes from within, from the soul. Its source is from that which is within and behind the mind, the heart, and the bodily expression. It is veiled and not fully realized in most of us. That is why psychic love is not easily manifested. We may realize mentally that love is a divine principle, feel it emotionally in our hearts and in physical yearnings. But the pure power of psychic love to heal us and transform our lives transcends all other love; if we knew its secrets, we could render ourselves beyond the reach of disease or disturbance. We should realize and manifest it in harmony with our mental, emotional, and physical conditions and needs. It is in this way that we correlate and give irresistible force to the divine healing power of love integrally in all planes of our being.

To have psychic love, and to possess its healing power, it is necessary to experience mystical union with the divine. Some individuals approach God through knowledge, others make a beginning by the path of action, but the quickest and most effective is the way of devotion. The Hindus call this Bhakti. This is the ecstasy of the Islamic Sufis. In the Old Testament it is David dancing for joy before the Lord, and in the New Testament the ecstasy of the early Christians which was such that they were thought to be drunken men. All these paths are fused together in the perfect union with the divine—the paths of knowledge, works, and love. This is the integral approach. But those who are in need of immediate help and the healing power from above should begin with the path of psychic love. They may sing in their hearts songs of love for God, in this fashion and phrased in their own way:

> *I have awaited Your word and Your presence O Lord,*
> *Quiet now, spilled of all demand,*
> *Content that there is none but You*
> *Joyous that all is You.*

> *Reveal Thyself to one who loves You*
> *Be my constant companion*
> *Do not leave my side*
> *Or depart from my heart.*

> *If you are gone, I am lost*
> *If you are present, I am found*

If you speak, I listen
If you are silent, I cannot hear

Rise, O Divine Victor and conquer in me
Make me strong to be ever in Your ways
To bind myself on the altar of Your love
There to kindle and consume
All that is spurned by You.

Let the bruises of the past and the unholy
Be burnt to ashes and their flame and smoke
Rise as a symbol of sacrifice to You.
Let me stand before Your altar perfect

Living as You live
Joyful as You are joyful
Loving as You love
Victorious as You are victorious,
Eternal as You are eternal.

It is this psychic or soul love that unites us with the Divine and is the key to the full expression of the healing power.

What is the secret of psychic love? It is to live inwardly rather than always in the external. In this way we evoke the power of the soul force within, united with the divine power above to fend off any illness which seeks to penetrate our bodily defenses or which may have already gained a hold upon us in some area of the body. We must be aware that these illnesses are like hostile armies ever on the alert to invade us when we permit any weaknesses in our being or become fearful of them. These hostile forces are the symbolic devils, the expressions of evil and hate, which Jesus cast out during his healing ministry. As we begin to live more and more inwardly, to develop more and more our psychic power, that power develops its own early warning system. It recognizes at once the first feelers of an attack of illness. Without excitement or anxiety, it calmly repulses them in the full assurance of its power to do so. This is important because it is easier to stop diseases before they enter than to throw them out once they have gotten inside.

How does this psychic love express itself in the healing process which I have described? How do we recognize it? The expression of love in the body is health. Love pours forth the radiant glance, the strong and graceful movement, the courageous rejection and defeat of all illness. The healing vibrations of inner love pervade all parts of our being with a harmonious sweetness that has a double charm and effect. First, it relaxes, soothes, and calms the cells and elements of the body in a way that medical science does not yet fully understand. Second, it pushes out of the body all the lingering malefactions of hate, pride, anger, and greed which are a chief mainspring of illness.

The next question that arises is from whence does psychic

love originate? It comes from that surrender to God's will which immediately takes the burden and the tension of healing away from our struggling human will and brings peace and calm confidence to the individual being. If this surrender is sincere and if we believe in the power of divine love for us to express itself in our healing, we will be healed. All our physical ailments will disappear. Our energy will be replenished and our health restored. What happens when our physical conditions begin to distress us? Ordinarily our mind turns at once to the doctor and medications, and sometimes we must avail ourselves of these aids. But if we have learned to surrender ourselves entirely to God, then our whole being enters immediately into the mighty power of divine love and harmony and all indispositions will cease. The healing power of love has no injurious side effects, no possibility of dangerous and unknown reactions. It is sure in its action and beneficial in all its results. It does more than cure. It re-creates.

Psychic love never expresses itself in pessimism. It does not resign itself to illness but seeks victory over it. There are some people who are capable of being cheerful and full of faith while enduring serious or chronic illness. Theirs is a victory but not the highest victory. It is a conquest within but not without. They have obtained a certain poise but not the external victory over disease which is necessary. Our aim should be not to capitulate, not to be a resigned sufferer, but to conquer the illness and to possess vibrant health and full vigor.

Why are we placing so much stress on the expression of psychic love for healing? It is because human love, while beautiful and effective as a healing power, is limited compared to divine love. Human love at its brightest glory is but a pale reflection of divine love. This is because our human instrumentalities are subject to human infirmities. Human love is sometimes restricted, expressed only toward family and friends. Sometimes such a love even omits the divine. But those persons whom we deem the happiest, the most peaceful and enlightened, have entered into communion with the love of God which includes all and excludes none. They see God in all men and in all things, and love him wherever he is and in all that he does. He who loves God in this way has no fear, and being fearless is the victor over illness. Such persons can bravely face and overcome every misfortune and illness because in these, too, they see the hand of God shaping, molding, and purifying them, leading them to an earthly perfection and an immortal life. They are like spiritual magnets which attract others to them. They uplift the spirits and heal the bodies of those who associate with them. A veritable halo is around their faces. In all their ways they are a force for the good, righteousness, and healing of mankind. In the New Testament, James says, "Is there anyone among you suffering? Let him pray. Is anyone among you sick? Let him call for the elders of the church, and let them pray over him, anointing him with oil in the name of the Lord. And the prayer of faith will save the sick and the Lord will raise him up . . . pray for one another that you may be healed. The prayer of a righteous man avails much."[39] So as James says, to be healed there must be an expression, a prayer, offered up to God and this expression of prayer must be for others so that you may be healed yourself.

Why is it that you cannot be healed unless you pray for others? It is because the individual can be perfected only if humanity is perfected. That is why Jesus died on the cross. That is why Buddha turned his back on the threshold of Nirvana, saying he would not cross it until he could take all men with him. As Paul said, "We are members one of another."[40] If one member is sick the whole body is ill. What is an epidemic if it is not a sickness of humanity and not an individual disease? Are we as individuals immune from disease if the collectivity is diseased? Illnesses are not only physical, but also mental and emotional, not only individual but communal and social as well. The collectivity must be healed as well as the individual. Those who think only of healing themselves will always be sick. When Jesus said, "Those who are well have no need of a physician, but those who are sick. I did not come to call the righteous, but sinners, to repentance,"[41] he was referring not only to physical illness but to the illness of ignorance, egoism, and evil in the world, to which he gave the name of sin. By repentance he meant to turn around and see the world in a different way. He was a physician not only to the physically sick but to humanity sick from any cause, not only to the individual but to the world and to the least of those in the world. This was his expression of divine love in healing.

We have pointed out that such divine love is the true expression of healing, how it is possible to express it, and to whom and to what it should be extended. We have stressed that no one is perfectly healed for herself alone but only if she prays for another, and that another is all of humanity, all of its suffering, distress, and of whatever nature that distress may be. This is universal healing from which none is omitted, for God is in all and his healing power is intended for all and for every purpose. Let us then pray to God in this way:

> *Let Divine peace and the knowledge of truth be given to us all. Let the vision of all men be clear; bring quiet and calm into our lives and dispel our needless anxieties. Let us cease to consider ourselves only, let us find the bliss of dedicating ourselves to the purposes of the Divine Will. Let the Glory of God be beautiful and his love expressed in all humanity. Let God's Kingdom on Earth continue to unfold until it is expressed and manifested in the lives of all and in the world in purity and perfection now and forever.*

NOTES

1 *New Revised Standard Version Bible*, Luke 17:19.

2 Ambalal Balkrishna Purani, *The Life of Sri Aurobindo*, 321.

3 *NRSV*, Luke 7:9.

4 *NRSV*, 2 Samuel 10:12.

5 *The Holy Bible: The New King James Version*, Matthew 10:16–26.

6 Sri Aurobindo, *Bases of Yoga*, 68–69.

7 *NKJV*, Luke 12:32.

8 *NKJV*, Ezekiel 11:19–20.

9 *NKJV*, Proverbs 28:1.

10 *NKJV*, Job 1:12.

11 *NKJV*, Job 12:1–3.

12 *The Holy Bible, King James Version*, Job 1:6–7.

13 *NRSV*, Job 40:1–2.

14 Sri Aurobindo, *Bases of Yoga*, 45–46.

15 *NRSV*, Job 40:10–14.

16 *NRSV,* Matthew 11:28–30.

17 *NKJV,* 1 Timothy 5:18.

18 *The Holy Bible: Revised Standard Version,* 2 Thessalonians 3:10.

19 *NKJV,* Matthew 6:28.

20 *NKJV,* Psalm 139: 8–10.

21 *KJV,* John 18:36.

22 *KJV,* 2 Timothy 2:15.

23 *KJV,* Psalm 90:17.

24 Sri Aurobindo, *Essays on the Gita,* XXII.

25 Philip Birnbaum, *Ethics of the Fathers,* 3:19.

26 *NKJV,* Romans 8:28–30.

27 *NRSV,* Ephesians 4:26–27.

28 Sri Aurobindo, *Integral Yoga,* 284.

29 *NRSV,* 1 Corinthians 10:13.

30 Sri Aurobindo, *Bases of Yoga,* III.

31 Sri Aurobindo, *Bases of Yoga,* II.

32 *NKJV,* Luke 7:47–50.

33 *NKJV,* 1 John 3:2–3.

34 *KJV,* Matthew 5:48.

35 *KJV,* 1 Corinthians 2:9.

36 *NRSV,* Mark 10:18.

37 *NKJV,* Luke 12:32.

38 Philip Birnbaum, *Ethics of the Fathers,* 5:18.

39 *NKJV,* James 5:13–16.

40 *NRSV,* Romans 12:5.

41 *NKJV,* Mark 2:17.

BIBLIOGRAPHY

Aurobindo, Sri. *Bases of Yoga*. Pondicherry: Sri Aurobindo Ashram, 1981.

———. *Essays on the Gita*. Pondicherry: Sri Aurobindo Ashram, 1987.

———. *Integral Yoga*. Twin Lakes, WI: Lotus Press, 2007.

———. *Prayers and Meditations of the Mother*. Pondicherry: Sri Aurobindo Ashram, 1948.

Birnbaum, Philip, ed. *Ethics of the Fathers*: Pirke Avot. Whitefish, MT: Literary Licensing LLC, 2013.

Farstad, Arthur, ed. *Holy Bible: The New King James Version*. Nashville, TN: Thomas Nelson, 1982.

The Holy Bible: The Authorized King James Version. New York: Abradale Press Publishers, 1959.

The Holy Bible: Revised Standard Version Containing the Old and New Testaments with the Apocrypha/Deuterocanonical Books. Iowa Falls, IA: World Bible Publishers, 1973.

Lao Tzu. *Tao Te Ching.* Trans. Jonathan Star. New York: Penguin Group, 2001.

Metzger, Bruce M., ed. *New Revised Standard Version Bible.* New York: Oxford University Press, 1989.

Purani, Ambalal Balkrishna. *The Life of Sri Aurobindo.* Pondicherry: Sri Aurobindo Ashram, 1978.

Rishabhchand. *In the Mother's Light.* Pondicherry: Sri Aurobindo Ashram, 1967.

Solomon, Norman, ed. *The Talmud.* New York: Penguin Classics, 2009.

INDEX

Aaron (biblical), 128
action/inaction problem, 53–55
Angels, 140
animal sacrifice, 117, 120
anti-Semitism, 105–7
anxiety, 23
Apostolic Christian Temple, xii
Arizona State University, xiii
art, 57–59
attention, 3–5
attitude, 45–46
Aurobindo, Sri
    on cultivating strength, 20
    on Divine Truth, 127
    on overcoming guilt, 111–12,
      124
    on power of faith, 17
    on seeking perfection, 138
    on spiritual obstacles, 28

Bhagavad Gita, xxi, 55
Bhakti, 150
Bible
    on guilt, 101
    and Pentecostalism, xi
    on perfection, 137–38, 142, 144
    on personal guilt, 110–11
    on psychic free will, 80
    and sacrifice theology, 117
    on Satan, 37
    on theological guilt, 104
    on worldly stress and suffering, 34
blind faith, 16–17
Buddha and Buddhism
    and collective healing, 155
    and Divine Will, 63
    and forgiveness, 115
    and inner purification, 90
    and inner work, 57

Buddha and Buddhism (*cont.*)
  and overcoming hostile forces, 29
  and sacrifice theology, 117
  and search for perfection, 140–41
  and sin and guilt, 103
  and theological guilt, 124

Calvin, John, 68
Catholicism, xvii, 105–7
Charismatic congregations, xvii
charity, 120
Christianity
  and author's background, x–xvi
  and forgiveness, 115, 116–17,
    123–25
  and overcoming hostile forces, 29
chronic illness, 148
civil rights, 72–73
collective difficulties, 31
communion with God, 144
confession, 120
Confucianism, 90, 124
consciousness, 12
contentment, 24
cooperation, 7–9
cosmic consciousness, 44
Cosmic Divine, 44
criminology, 125

David (biblical), 150
depression, 20
determinism of nature, 75–76
difficulties, 20–21
disease, 8–9. *See also* healing
divinatory arts, xix, 34
Divine Commander, 12
Divine Consciousness
  descent into the physical, 11–13
  mastery of, 15–17
  and spiritual healing, 17
Divine Force
  and cultivation of inner strength, 21
  and Divine Will, 62
  and overcoming hostile forces, 50
  and receptivity, 4

  and sincerity, 4
  and spiritual healing, 16
Divine Grace
  and cultivation of inner strength, 20
  and overcoming hostile forces, 28
  and retention, 5
Divine Incarnation, 118
Divine Light
  and overcoming hostile forces, 47
  and psychic free will, 81
Divine Love, 127–28, 133, 153–56
Divine Science, xi
Divine Truth
  and Divine Will, 62
  and forgiveness, 127–29
  and inner work, 55–56
  and self-sacrifice, 90
Divine Will
  and cooperation, 8
  and psychic free will, 81
  and psychic love, 153, 156
  and work, 61–63
dual consciousness, 61–62

economics, 72
Ecumenical Council, 105
ego
  and free will, 75–77
  and inner work, 55
  and overcoming hostile forces, 49–50
  and psychic love, 155
  and sacrifice, 93–95
  and search for perfection, 141
Elisha (biblical), 5
epilepsy, 148
evangelists, 16
evil, 31
evolution, 30, 76, 86–87, 140
Ezekiel (biblical), 31

faith, 3, 16–17, 38
Fillmore, Charles, xi
Fillmore, Myrtle, xi
First Church of Religious Science, xiii
forgiveness

and dangers of ignorance, 123–25
and divine truth, 127–29
from the heart, 119–21
and personal guilt, 112
and spiritual purification, 131–33
understanding, 115–18
Fourth Lateran Council, 106–7
free will
  egoistic, 75–77
  and the partisan mind, 71–73
  psychic, 79–81
  reconciling with Divine Will, 67–69
Free Will Baptists, 68
frustration, 23

Goddard, Neville, xi, xvi
Gospels, xxi
The Green Pastures (play), 140
guilt
  defining guilt, 99–101
  immorality of theological guilt, 103–4
  and modern psychology, 123
  removing personal guilt, 109–12
  removing theological guilt, 105–8

Hall, Manly P., xiv–xv
Harris, Obadiah, ix–xv, xv–xx, xx–xxii
healing
  and author's background, xvii
  and Divine Consciousness, 12
  and the partisan mind, 72
  and passivity, 8–9
  and psychic love, 152–53, 152–56
Hebraic law, 54
Higher Consciousness
  and cultivation of inner strength,
    20–21
  and sacrifice, 91
higher education, xiii
Hinduism
  and psychic love, 150
  and theological guilt, 124
Holmes, Ernest, xi, xii, xiv, 145
Horowitz, Mitch, xxi
hostile forces

and advancing spiritual consciousness,
  45–47
and author's background, xviii–xx
defeating, 49–50
and divine life on Earth, 29–31
and life beyond stress and suffering,
  33–35
and obstacles to spiritual growth, 27–28
and psychic love, 152
strengthening weaknesses, 41–44
upending hostile forces, 37–39
human reason, 68–69, 71–72

ignorance
  and crucifixion of Christ, 124
  and definitions of guilt, 101
  and forgiveness, 117, 123–25, 129, 132
  and personal guilt, 110
  and theological guilt, 103
illness
  and cultivation of inner strength, 19–21
  and Divine consciousness, 11–13
  and psychic love, 152–53
immortality, 95
individual difficulties, 31
indulgences, 120
inner self
  and cultivation of inner strength, 20–21
  and frustration and anxiety, 23–24
  and inner work, 57–59, 62–63
  and strength, 19–21
Innocent the Third, pope, 106–7
intellectual rigor, xv–xvi
Islam, xviii, 106–7, 150

James (biblical), 144, 154–55
James, William, xvii
Jesus
  crucifixion, 105–6, 123–24, 131,
    132–33
  and divine life on Earth, 29–30
  and Divine Will, 62, 63
  and faith, 3
  and forgiveness, 112, 116–17, 118,
    121, 123–24, 128, 131

Jesus (*cont.*)
   and inner work, 57–58
   and obstacles to spiritual growth, 27–28
   and overcoming hostile forces, 50
   and perfection, 137, 144–45
   and psychic love, 152
   and sacrifice, 90, 95
   and search for perfection, 146
   and spiritual healing, 17
   transfiguration of, 144
Job (biblical)
   and Divine consciousness, 12
   and obstacles to spiritual growth, 27
   and overcoming hostile forces, 41–43, 50
   and upending hostile forces, 37–39
Job, Book of, 37, 39, 42
John (biblical), 133, 144
Judaism, xvi, xviii, 105–6, 115–16
judicial codes, xvi

karma, 68
knowledge, 149–50
Kol Nidre, 115–16

laying-on of hands, 16–17
learning, 147–48
"left hand of God," 42
love
   Divine Love, 127–28, 133, 153–56
   and perfection, 137–46
   psychic love, 147–56

maleficent forces, xviii–xx
medical science, 13, 15. *See also* healing
messianism, 31
metaphysics
   and author's background, xi, xii, xix
   and hostile forces, 42
   and search for perfection, 146
miracles, xvii, 12
misfortune, 112
missionary work, 68
mistakes, 99–101
Mohammad, 90

Moses (biblical), 90
Muslims, 106–7
mystery religions, xix

Nazis, 107
Needleman, Jacob, xxi
New Mexico State University, xiii
New Testament, 11, 144, 150, 154
New Thought movement, xi, xii, xv–xvi
Nirvana, 155

occult practices, xix, 34
Old Testament, 27, 150
omnipotence, 67, 68
Omnipresent Divine, 55–56
original sin, 107–8, 123

partisanship, 71–73
passivity, 7, 8–9
patience, 12
Paul (biblical)
   and Divine Will, 62
   on forgiveness, 112
   on inner work, 57
   and the partisan mind, 73
   and the problem of action/inaction, 54–55
   and psychic free will, 81
   and psychic love, 148–49, 155
   and theological guilt, 104
   and "thorn in the flesh" passage, 148–49
penal codes, 103
Penitentes, 120
Pentecostalism, x–xi, xvii
perfection, 137–46
persistence, 12, 33
pessimism, 153
Peter (biblical), 144
Philosophical Research Society, xiv
Pontius Pilate, 57
practice, 85–86
prayer, xxi, 120
predestination, 68, 81
Presbyterian church, 67–68

preventive medicine, 13
primitive Baptists, 68
Psalms, 55, 63
psychic free will, 79–81
psychic love, 147–56
psychology
    and author's background, xx–xxi
    and criminal theory, 125
    and forgiveness, 121, 123
    and psychological health, 16
    and theological guilt, 107
    and worldly stress and suffering, 35
purification, 89–92

rabbinical scholars, 147
racial discrimination, 104, 105
receptivity, 3–5
religious politics, xv
retention, 4–5
Roberts, Oral, x–xi
Roman Empire, 90–91

sacrifice
    and forgiveness, 116–17
    and inner purification, 89–92
    and rejection of ego, 93–95
    and self-consciousness, 85–87
Satan, 37–38
Schweitzer, Albert, 29
science, 72, 80
Science of Mind movement, xi, xii, xiii,
    145
Second Corinthians 12:7, 148
The Secret Teachings of All Ages (Hall), xiv
segregationism, 104
self-awareness, 85–87, 139
self-determination, 86–87
self-healing, 3–4
self-knowledge, 28
selflessness, 139
self-mortification, 120–21
self-sufficiency, xxi
self-transcendence, 86–87
sickness, 141–42. *See also* healing; illness
signs and wonders, xvii

sin, 103, 131
sincerity, 3–5, 119–21, 143
soul
    and free will, 79–81
    and psychic love, 149–52
    and sacrifice, 93, 94
    and search for perfection, 142,
        145–46
spiritual consciousness, 45–47, 85
spiritual healing, 15
spiritual immunization, 13
spiritual purification, 131–33
statism, 95
stress, 35, 43, 46
suffering, 33–35
Sufism, 150
Supreme Divine Knowledge, 94

Tagore, Rabindranath, 145
Talmud, 81, 128–29, 147
Taoism, 45, 138
Tao Te Ching, xxi
televangelists, x–xi
theological guilt, 103–4, 124
Thoreau, Henry David, 34
transformation, 143
transformative sacrifice, 89–92

understanding, 115–18
Unity, xi
University of Michigan, xiii
University of Philosophical Research, xv

Vedas, xvi
vigilance, 44

Will of God. *See* Divine Will
work
    and Divine Will, 61–63
    and inner progress, 57–59
    and the problem of action/inaction,
        53–56
World War II, 107

Yom Kippur, 115–16

ABOUT THE AUTHOR

OBADIAH HARRIS is the founder and president of the University of Philosophical Research (www.UPRS.edu), an accredited distance-learning university that grants graduate degrees in consciousness studies and transformational psychology, and undergraduate degrees in liberal studies. The school is built upon the intellectual traditions of independent scholar of religion Manly P. Hall (1901–1990), who founded its landmark Los Angeles campus, the Philosophical Research Society. Also president of the Philosophical Research Society, Harris has had a long career in both mainstream academia and the American metaphysical culture. He was an understudy of Dr. Haridas Chaudhuri (1913–1975), founder of the California Institute of Integral Studies (CIIS), and holds a PhD in education administration and supervision from the University of Michigan and an MA in education from Arizona State University, where he was an associate professor of education and director of community education. For almost two decades at Arizona State he designed programs in community outreach and in adult and continuing education. Harris has held numerous ministerial pulpits and collaborated with figures of major influence in contemporary spirituality, including Ernest Holmes (1887–1960). Born in northeastern Oklahoma, he lives in Los Angeles.